Richard Abbey

Christian Cradlehood

Religion in the Nursery

Richard Abbey

Christian Cradlehood
Religion in the Nursery

ISBN/EAN: 9783337371395

Printed in Europe, USA, Canada, Australia, Japan

Cover: Foto ©Lupo / pixelio.de

More available books at **www.hansebooks.com**

CHRISTIAN CRADLEHOOD;

OR,

Religion in the Nursery.

By R. ABBEY,

Author of "Diuturnity," "Ecce Ecclesia," "City of God," "Church and Ministry," "Baptismal Demonstrations," "Divine Assessment," "Call to the Ministry," and several smaller works.

NASHVILLE, TENN.
SOUTHERN METHODIST PUBLISHING HOUSE.
PRINTED FOR THE AUTHOR.
1881

Contents.

Introductory Essay.. 7

CHAPTER I.
Concerning the Natural Rights of Children.. 20

CHAPTER II.
The Great Law of Morals............................ 24

CHAPTER III.
Concerning the Religious State of Children at Birth.. 29

CHAPTER IV.
Of the Imbecile, or Infantile, Period............ 33

CHAPTER V.
Happiness is Always the Result of Obedience.. 41

CHAPTER VI.
Common Parental Cruelties......................... 46

CHAPTER VII.
Too Late, Too Late................................... 50

CHAPTER VIII.
Children Must be Broken............................ 56

CHAPTER IX.
Obedience is not Slavish............................ 61

CHAPTER X.
Thoughtless Training................................. 67

CHAPTER XI.
Whipping Children.. 71

CHAPTER XII.
A Threatening Government.. 79

CHAPTER XIII.
Honor and Manliness in Children.............................. 85

CHAPTER XIV.
The Religious Capacity of Children............................ 89

CHAPTER XV.
The Religious Capacity of Children (*continued*).... 100

CHAPTER XVI.
Childhood is Natural and Normal............................... 109

CHAPTER XVII.
The High Parental Relation....................................... 114

CHAPTER XVIII.
Eligibility to Church-Membership............................. 122

CHAPTER XIX.
What is the Age of Religious Capability?.................. 134

CHAPTER XX.
Early Ideas of Religion.. 140

CHAPTER XXI.
Is Sin Ever Necessary?.. 149

CHAPTER XXII.
The Fickleness of Childhood..................................... 157

CHAPTER XXIII.
Children Growing Up Sinless..................................... 162

CONTENTS.

CHAPTER XXIV.
Loving and Fearing God.................................... 169

CHAPTER XXV.
Conversion, or New Birth............................... 176

CHAPTER XXVI.
Child's Faith and Conversion......................... 183

CHAPTER XXVII.
Children Once Converted................................. 191

CHAPTER XXVIII.
Conversion—Joining Church............................. 196

CHAPTER XXIX.
Of Child's Faith... 204

CHAPTER XXX.
The Right Time for Conversion....................... 214

CHAPTER XXXI.
Of Church-membership..................................... 222

CHAPTER XXXII.
On the Baptizing of Children......................... 231

CHAPTER XXXIII.
A Remedy... 234

CHAPTER XXXIV.
A Practical Suggestion..................................... 239

CHAPTER XXXV.
The Lord's Supper.. 249

Conclusion 255

CHRISTIAN CRADLEHOOD.

INTRODUCTORY ESSAY.

SINCE improvement in all human affairs is professedly, and ought to be really, the great business and effort of all men, it would seem surprising that sometimes so little attention is paid to its early stages. Nothing can be well built that is faulty in its foundation. Civil government, laws, commerce, religion, churches, education, health, literature, science, medicine, agriculture, railroads, navigation, morals, and public and private good of all kinds, are to-day what they are, for the most part, if not almost or quite wholly, because of the well or ill-directed attention, or non-attention, which was paid to cradle-life a few years ago. Schools, and what is commonly called education, form a valuable and important factor in life, but they cannot work beyond their natural domain. Character is well set before their services are required.

The nursery is the *nursery* of life. That which is not prepared there is not prepared at all. Many things may live, but nothing has healthful thrift without well-directed nursery labors. Nothing social, moral, or industrial, can thrive without it. Christianity itself limps, and is inefficient without a healthful nursery.

Nine-tenths of all the preaching is lost. What a waste of power! No such waste is seen elsewhere in all the industries and economies of life. And is this beyond the reach of remedy? While there is abundance of general measures of relief proposed, and improvement here and there is constantly urged, I am not aware of any specific, practical remedy being recommended for the relief in question. There is a remedy for all waste, but frequently it is either not clearly seen, or, if seen, is not within convenient reach. But such is not the case here. In this case a remedy is in plain view, but only to those who search for it carefully.

Let us suppose a hundred persons to be preached to the ensuing year who are over fifteen years old. They are of the better sort. For the most part they have had religious parents. They have a respectful veneration for the Church and its religion, and partially keep the Sabbath, revere the Bible, and respect the ministry.

Now let us look at those persons at the close of the year. They have been habitual church-goers, observing generally all the decencies of such occasions. They have heard from thirty to fifty or a hundred sermons, besides attending a number of prayer-meetings, and have generally expended their opinions—no mean ones—about the preaching, doctrines, style, etc. They have furnished pecuniary support to the Church to half the extent of the Church-members. They "don't belong to the Church."

Now, what has been the effect of the year's preaching on these people? Let us see. About four or five have joined the Church, as it is called, and two or three of these give fair promise of religious life. This is about the average of our preaching—from two to five converts out of every hundred per year. We probably fall below it more frequently than we rise above it.

Half our converts are from persons who seldom hear preaching. Thousands of thousands of persons attend church with some regularity, or at least frequently, all the days of a long irreligious life. Many persons attend preaching year after year with no serious idea or remote expectation of becoming religious. Fifty sermons and forty prayer-meetings to the convert is not generally considered very discouraging. These sermons generally set forth the gospel with no ordinary talent. Preaching has greatly improved of late years. Such preaching as that of Wesley, Calvin, Massillon, and Watson, is very common now everywhere.

These hearers, too, are not mere idle listeners. They admire and feel the force of the powerful and stirring appeals and reasoning to which they listen. They are oftentimes moved to the bottom, and scores and hundreds are the half-way, or "almost," resolves they make in all honest fidelity, but, as the treacherous future discloses, only to be violated as fast as made.

Under our preaching the Church holds its own, and gains a little. One would suppose that the incessant labors of a hundred thousand picked men, embodying much of the best talent and learning of mankind, would effect something, directed to almost any subject, good or bad, true or false.

Surely there is something out of joint here. Such waste of labor is not seen in any other field. The disproportion of labor and result, so far as result can be seen and estimated, shows a loss of power ten, if not a hundred, fold greater than in other enterprises.

Suppose the subject-matter of argument and exhortation, with so little objection to any thing put forth, related to improved modes of agriculture, or to education. Suppose these vast labors of zeal, eloquence, and logical reasoning, related to greatly improved modes of securing larger and more advantageous civil liberty and the lightening of civil burdens, to new and improved methods of conducting commerce, or to sanitary processes by which health and longevity would be largely secured, or to any thing promising large increase of human advantage of any sort. It may be replied that these subjects have received and are receiving large polemical attention. This is true, but such debates are of a character very different from those under consideration. The former relate to the safest and most expeditious or best modes of reaching ends desired by all, while the latter are almost wholly expostulatory exhortations to acknowledged duty and conceded advantage. Men debate about the best modes of securing the largest and safest civil liberty, but they do not debate, by the thousand, and at great labor and cost, whether they will *have* civil liberty at all. Men do not debate for and against commerce, or education, or science—whether we should have such things at all. Nobody argues, by the thousand, that we ought to have medicine, or government, or literature, or navigation. No such arguments are needed.

The one hundred persons above alluded to do not entertain views or opinions different from those of the ministers to whom they listen. With no difference of creed or opinion, they do not argue back—they all think alike. Sermons thus unheeded and neglected are not answered with No, no, but with Yes, yes.

Now, *why* this vast waste of power? Why so little result from such immense labor? The usual answer is that the great wickedness of mankind is the cause. We have inherited so much wickedness from Adam that men are very wicked. This is a reply, but not an answer. Wicked men generally, in other matters, do listen to reason, and change their course on being convinced of a better course.

It is true that wickedness is but another name for irreligion, but it is also true that great mistakes are frequently made about our inheriting all this from Adam. The truth is we inherited none of it from Adam. Adam furnished us with nothing but the seed. We ourselves cultivated the seed, and raised the crop. Seed do but little if any harm uncultivated. Wickedness is not inherited. *We make it ourselves.* We inherit a tendency to wickedness, and by failing or neglecting to resist the tendency we become wicked.

The ancestral inheritance of evil was seed, or tendency. Vice or virtue have seeds, or tendencies. This does no harm of itself. Seed may be cultivated, or be permitted to grow, and so may a tendency. This evil inheritance has been increased by our own cultivation a thousand-fold. At five or ten years it was increased a hundred-fold, and at twenty-five a thousand-fold. And so, as we preach only to persons over ten years, and mostly to those over twenty, our preaching is directed in but an almost infinitesimal degree against our inherited evil. Almost wholly it is applied not to inherited, but to cultivated, evil.

In other words, under our system of practical culture and ministering the gospel, we direct our batteries to the extent of ninety-nine hundredths of our force against fortifications of our own erection; or if we did not build these fortifications with our own hands, we stood passively by and, without objection, saw Satan do it. Now, why not bring the gospel to bear against the enemy's works before these strong walls of defense are grown up at all? Why wait for manhood and womanhood, or even youthhood? Why not begin at the first?

Ordinary nursery training and Sunday-schools do not by any means meet the case. If properly conducted they become subsidiary helps. But these things do not begin until the fifth or tenth year, when the character is well set, and very difficult to change. So when we begin to present the gospel remedy, the power of evil is augmented twenty or forty-fold. Now, why not apply this gospel remedy at the first, before this great increase has become added? Why wait until the enemy has so greatly strengthened his works? or why not begin before these evil powers have strengthened at all? We seldom begin with a fair hope and good expectation of conversion and Church-membership before children reach ten or fifteen years. Indeed, our very books which teach and treat of early Christian training speak of, or encourage, the idea that conversion at the age of ten or fifteen is early conversion! Why not so plan and arrange our ministerial work as to look for and secure conversion the third year, or the second year, or the first year?

Now, of the Christian man who considers that either impracticable or difficult, I have this to say: He did not get his Christian teaching from either Scripture or from sound philosophy, but from passively following a social morbid fashion.

The following essay advocates the expediency, practicability, and necessity of beginning at the beginning—that is, to let the Christian life take an even start with the natural life. It holds the first year to be more important for the solid implantation of Christian principle than any subsequent year, and so of the second, the third, the fourth. It explains and advises an even start in the race of life. The general rule is that, disobedience having several years the start, it is seldom overtaken. Church-preaching alone is a demonstrated failure. We build up difficulties mountain-high, or, what is about the same thing, stand by and see them grow up, putting forth no hand of resistance, and spend life, labor, and talent, in vain attempts to batter them down.

We neglect the rich virgin soil, and then vainly try to cultivate the worn-out lands. The agriculturist who begins to cultivate the tender herbage when the weeds have attained ten times their height may labor hard, late and early, but his crop will be small and sickly. Just so of children-culture. In both cases the failure will be certain unless we *begin at the beginning*.

The corn-fields of two farmers, alike at the planting, were cultivated differently. The one farmer was there with his implements as soon as the corn was up. Weeds were abundant, but they were tender, and easily removed; the corn never felt their choking influence. The labor was light and the harvest abundant. Not so with neighbor Indulgence. He waited a full month because, as it then seemed, the weeds did not impede the growth of the corn very much. But soon after the corn began to dwindle and turn yellow. The weeds grew much faster than was anticipated. The farmer toiled hard and faithfully, late and early, and really did much more work than his neighbor, but his harvest was sickly, meager, and profitless.

There are points of fundamental defect in our cradle and nursery culture. In theory we tacitly concede that young children are not capable of Christianity—that they can only be trained for it after awhile.

The following theses are advocated in this essay:

First. Christianity being exactly adapted to all sane persons, in all circumstances, ages, and conditions, it is an error to exclude children from its highest benefits and highest responsibilities because of tender age — any age.

Second. Idiots and insane persons are incapable of Christianity; but not, however, because they are intellectually incapable of understanding the system of divine salvation, but because they are not capable of obedience.

Third. Christianity is obedience to rightful authority, and nothing more — ready, implicit obedience.

Fourth. Capability of doing wrong implies capability to do right, which is Christianity in the highest sense.

Fifth. The earliest moral or intellectual impulse of which a child is capable is affectionate obedience; hence, as the earlier the more favorable is the period for the formation and permanent planting of habit, so the earlier the more favorable the period for the solid implantation of sound religious principle and practice. This early opportunity once lost is seldom regained.

Sixth. Affectionate obedience to rightful authority is not irksome, unpleasant, or disagreeable in any persons of any age, if it be taught and cultivated from birth; but in all cases when so encouraged and fixed as a principle, it is pleasant, agreeable, and furnishes the highest cheerfulness and happiness in life. There is no reluctance in true obedience.

Seventh. As sin is not, and can *never be, necessary,* so it is always avoidable, and ought to be avoided. And as the gospel is the only cure for sin, it ought to be prominently, formidably, and effectually brought to bear upon the earliest periods of cradlehood, because wrong-doing in some shapes begins from the very first, and repetitions of any thing greatly increase the tendency thereto.

Eighth. While character in a man is never entirely fixed and finished until about the close of life, its massive foundations are largely and almost immovably laid in the first two or three years of life.

If attention has not been well directed to the simplicity and naturalness of cradle and early nursery government by writers and teachers, it is high time it were done. It is not pretended that this little, humble treatise sets forth an elaborated system of this kind; but it is pretended that it contains some wholesome hints to parents and ministers in that direction. And it is hoped they may arrest the attention of some men or women of thought who may elaborate and popularize the subject. I cannot be mistaken in the belief that by some adequate and practical handling of the subject every social interest of mankind may be elevated a full octave in no great number of years. The *improvement of society* must begin here.

CHAPTER I.

CONCERNING THE NATURAL RIGHTS OF CHILDREN.

I THINK it safe to say that no class of persons amongst us are so generally and so largely deprived of their natural rights as children—those under ten years or so, and more especially those under about four or five.

Who excluded the Christian religion from the cradle and the nursery? and by what authority was it done? Does natural science or revealed truth authorize it? Surely not. It is a mere worldly, unsanctified custom.

The parent is appointed to do the child's thinking, direct his acting in all things, and start him, well equipped at every point, in the great warfare of life. The soft, passive, wax-like, living human person, unformed, but flexible and yielding, is put into the hands of the parent with the solemn injunction to control him in every thing, so that from this unknowing and unthinking little mass of humanity may grow a man or woman for life and for God. The obligation of the animal mother is to protect the offspring from outward violence, and supply physical wants. The human mother is to do more. Her obligation is to make a person and character out of living, but almost raw, material. The child has a natural right to this character. He needs it through life. He can scarcely live without it. It is the product not only of high obligation, but of labor, of love, and of care.

The usual way is, in case of failure—which is the case grossly in nine cases in ten, and partially in nearly all the rest—to put the blame on the child or on nature, but the guilty party is the parent always. It is the neglected child, the child deprived of his natural rights by the mother and the father, that encounters a degraded life of ignorance and vice. The parent prepared the way—either by doing, or not doing—for idleness, for dishonesty, for irreligion, and for crime. Quite likely the parents themselves were treated as badly in their childhood.

In the rearing of children, as in most other matters, we, with more or less thoughtlessness, "follow the fashion," and consider that if we come up to about the average of family culture, or perhaps some of us aim a little above it, we are doing tolerably well. We, all of us, look with far too much complacency and self-satisfaction upon average life and duties.

The obligation to supply the moral and religious wants of children is the highest obligation known to domestic life. And yet how woefully it is neglected! How little is it even thought of! Instead of a wise and prudent regard for the rights and interests of young children, the first few years are spent in fondling, play, and caressing exclusively, save the usual attention to physical wants. Moral culture is not thought of. And although these playful endearments and nursery pastimes are very important to both parent and child, yet if other duties of higher culture be at the same time neglected, the most serious consequences cannot fail to follow. Almost uniformly before the first lessons in moral training are attempted, the opportunity—the best and by far the most favorable opportunity—for their enforcement is gone, never to be regained.

The greatest of all misfortunes resting upon the social surface of Christendom to-day is this neglect of early training. By early training I mean training from the first. Most of this training lies in the first year, and most of that remaining in the second, and most of that remaining in the third, and so on.

Now, the reader who has studied so little of human nature as to "know better than all that," had better lay this little book aside, and read no farther. He is not likely to be profited by any thing it contains.

CHAPTER II.

THE GREAT LAW OF MORALS.

THERE is, after all, but one lesson and one law of morals and religion to be inculcated and observed from birth to the end of life. That lesson is *obedience—obedience to rightful authority.* That includes, implies, and combines, the whole of moral duty and moral principle. The only difference between right and wrong is obedience to proper authority on the one hand, and self-will — doing as one chooses — on the other. Obeying rightful authority is human perfectibility, applied at any stage of life, and in any circumstances of human condition, from birth to death. And it is a great mistake to suppose that any living person of sane mind, however young, is not fully capable of obedience, as much so as any other person.

A young child is not capable of understanding any reason for obedience, or the duty or advantages of it; but he fully understands its nature, and is as fully competent to the performance as he ever will be. His obedience is mere submission without a reason, and yet with him it carries all the ends and purposes of obedience with the highest and most affectionate motives. This infantile obedience can always be administered by the parent with the greatest ease and good nature in both parent and child, *if begun in time*. A word fitly spoken, not at all understood literally, is nevertheless well comprehended by its tone, or a look or gesture. The child does not know there are such words as command and obey, and yet no one understands these things better than he. Obedience is not necessarily accompanied by a virtuous wish to do right, but the young are so constituted that the absence of these moral motives detracts not a whit from all the advantages to be derived from the highest style of obedience to law.

So that obedience, yielding submission, non-resistance to rightful authority, understood or not understood, is the great comprehensive law of the moral universe. The Decalogue enjoins obedience, and nothing more. Thou shalt, thou shalt not, are its behests. God requires obedience to rightful authority, and nothing more. Every thing that is right is obedience—every thing that is wrong is disobedience. Obedience secures the highest liberty of man—disobedience entails the most slavish degradation. Implicit obedience to rightful authority forms the sole platform of all morals and all religion.

Some persons are too young to recognize God as the rightful superior, but none are too young to recognize a superior. This transfer of authority from the parent to the Maker begins with the opening dawn of the intellect, and closes with the maturity of manhood.

It may be said that this mere obedience to parents is not religion. That may depend on the definition given to the term religion. It places him in a right relation to Christ, so the Saviour himself says: "Whosoever therefore shall humble himself as this little child, the same shall be greatest in the kingdom of heaven." Not because he was a child, but because he was a humble and obedient child.

The law of obedience being the great moral law of life and of universal application, and happiness being the end of man's creation, it follows necessarily that happiness is the measure of obedience, and obedience the measure of happiness. This law is absolutely universal. An unhappy child is unhappy because of his disobedience, and in exact proportion to his disobedience. And just so of an older person. A cheerful and happy child is cheerful and happy because of his obedience, and in exact proportion to the submission and unhesitating readiness of his obedience.

And so of liberty. Ignorance of life and its laws supposes that obedience restricts liberty and lessens happiness. That depends upon which code of laws is obeyed. There are two. Obedience to rightful authority produces the largest liberty, and the largest happiness, because it harmonizes with all nature around us; while obedience to wrongful authority produces the smallest liberty, and smallest measure of happiness, for the reason that it conflicts with the constitution of nature around us, and disturbs and deranges the sources of happiness.

God made things right, and not wrong. It is unreasonable to look for early piety where impiety has been regularly, if not systematically, inculcated from birth. Religion is the submission of the self-will; irreligion is the exercise and strengthening of it. A child, though he knows nothing of the moral aspects of these things, following the bent of his fallen nature, is suffered to have his own way in ten thousand little things, where there is a well-understood contest for supremacy, looked upon, it is true, as matter of mere trifle by the inconsiderate parent, but is none the less real on that account, necessarily becomes strengthened and strengthened more and more every day in the solid principles of legitimate infidelity. Then at the age of eight, ten, or fifteen years, it is expected that all this growth in infidelity shall be laid aside, and a spirit of submissive obedience and cross-bearing be adopted. This is unreasonable and unnatural. Such things do occur, but they are one in a hundred. The submission of the will, or cross-bearing, as it is also called, is a hundred-fold more easily inculcated the first year, and in the nursery, than ever after. If any one is unwilling to call this Christianity, he is at full liberty to call it by another name, but he cannot fail to see that it embodies all the principles of true religion.

It is very easy with any child of any disposition to establish this principle and practice of submission, if undertaken at the first, and pursued with some reasonable diligence; and it is very certain that to fail to do so is to anchor the principles of infidelity solidly, if not immovably. This is seen in a sad and uniform experience.

CHAPTER III.

CONCERNING THE RELIGIOUS STATE OF CHILDREN AT BIRTH.

IN a future chapter I shall have more to say on this subject, but will make a few preliminary observations here.

Religion consists in two things—first, what God does to and for us by his grace; and secondly, what man does for himself toward God in the resignation of his will and obedience of life. But as God requires of none beyond his capability, he supplies the young with more grace because they need more. According to several ability is the law of requirement.

Children are not born sinners, to speak accurately, because as yet they have not sinned for mere lack of capability. They are not walkers, for they have not walked, nor talkers, for they have not talked. But the natural tendency to either sinning or talking is the same. The one needs a preventive—the other does not. And the Christian religion is both preventive and cure of sin. The grace of God in

Christ is fully adequate to both those purposes, if properly applied.

And a great practical question is, When is the proper time to begin the practical application of the Christian religion to personal childhood for prevention, or for both prevention and cure, as any one may choose to have it? I say for both prevention and cure, for no man can tell precisely when a child first begins to commit sin.

And the answer to this question is, *At the very first*. There is no proper time to begin but at the very first. It is the revealed policy of the Almighty that the Christian religion should have direct and immediate application to all living persons. But it may be asked, Is not sin inevitable, and so a necessary and even an unavoidable thing?

Sin is to be avoided as well as cured. It is to be shunned, deprecated, hated, not courted or counseled with. To conclude that sin, prospectively considered, cannot be avoided, is to invite Satan to come and sit, and eat, and sleep with us, or at least to let him know that we expect him to do so. If we find ourselves compelled to look upon sin in the past as an unfortunate experience, let us apply to Christ for deliverance and for future preventive. But let no living man, from the birth to the grave, acknowledge that in any future moment Satan will be stronger than Christ.

Obedience is Christianity. A child of obedience is in the same position as a mature man of obedience. Complete obedience meets all moral requirements in young or old. There is a time when a child is not capable of moral obedience, but there is no time when he is not capable of actual obedience. And the habit of actual or of non-moral obedience may very easily be so well and so fully established that moral obedience, when the period of its exercise shall arrive, will be a delight rather than a burden. Moral accountability begins at an imperceptible minimum, and increases imperceptibly, and transfers itself by imperceptible stages from the earthly parent to the heavenly authority.

The child who is fully obedient—compulsory at first and moral afterward, being formed into a habit—is in the highest state of grace known to Christianity; not perhaps in respect of mere technical theology, but in acceptance or right position before God in Christ; for obedience to rightful authority is the highest moral state.

The strong and never-failing tendency to

sinfulness and ruin in children at birth, called by various names by different writers, will be inquired into hereafter; but in order that a child may enter into life with prospects brighter than very darkness, two things are indispensably necessary. First, by solemn prayer to the Saviour of children, he must be dedicated to God by special parental sanctification. He must be *set apart* from this unholy turmoil of strife and life, into which he would otherwise enter, to a Christian life and course of conduct such as Christ has provided for all children. Secondly, from the very first of life a habit and practice of ready obedience to parents must be thoroughly inaugurated and established; not a reluctant doing merely, by persuasion, or hire, or fear, but a cheerful, ready, and loving obedience. And, once established, it must be kept in fresh and lively exercise.

CHAPTER IV.

OF THE IMBECILE, OR INFANTILE, PERIOD.

THERE is a period of childhood of entire moral imbecility and ignorance of moral duty. We cannot mark its precise termination. So far as we know, it has no exact termination; but, extending from birth, it shades and blends very gradually and imperceptibly into the state of moral accountability. I suppose it may generally reach to a period not much beyond the close of the second year—generally, perhaps not so far. This period in the life of every person, which we might call his absolute nonage, is generally regarded an entire moral blank, or period of moral waste. For it is said, "What can you teach a child who has no perception of right and wrong? Training, or moral nurture, must be begun after awhile." So far from this period being a moral waste, and not susceptible of moral improvement, *I believe it to be by far the most important for moral and religious culture of any period of the same length in the whole life of the man.* And I here pause a minute or two for that expression to settle well in the mind of the reader. I attach great importance to the idea. I hold the first year the most important of all the years, and the first two years the most important of any two, the first three of any three, and so on. This belief may seem strange to some. If so, it is because you have not thought deeply and rightly on the subject.

Let it be repeated: the great fundamental principle of moral life—that which makes up all morals and all religion—that which both constitutes and supports every thing that is right, and stands in never-ending opposition to every thing that is wrong, in all states and all circumstances—is *obedience—obedience to rightful authority.* By this is meant not the mere actual doing for present reasons, but the doing from a spirit, temper, and character of submissive obedience. And let it be especially noted: this spirit of obedience in children is brought about in no other way than by constant training, custom, and habitual exercise. And farther, that this solid formation of habit, for obedience or disobedience, begins with inevitable certainty the first day of life, and proceeds with most wonderful power and rapidity. The first year settles the habit of obedience more than any other year, the first two more than any other two, the first three more than any other three, and so on.

Of course, a child of that age thinks and knows nothing about obedience as a moral duty. He knows nothing about a reason for any thing. He knows how to obey, and what obedience is, as well as he will know at forty. He forms a habit of obedience as easily and as readily as any other habit; and everybody knows that the earlier habits of any kind are formed, no matter how early, the stronger they are. It requires great effort to break off early habits of any kind. Indeed, generally, it cannot be done. They follow a man to the grave. The man in the Gospel said truly, "I cannot dig."

Many persons suppose some good degree of intelligence or moral perception is necessary in order to obedience. This is an error. A dog or horse is as capable of mere obedience as a habit as a child or a man. There is no intrinsic moral worth in obedience at this age, but its value is none the less on that account. Without it, and for the lack of it, nineteen persons in every twenty are ruined, world without end, even in our best communities, and the one in twenty is saved, if saved at all, by a most amazing miracle of mercy. It is the habit of obeying, and not the merit or goodness of it, of which I now write. Every mother knows that a child, no matter how young, forms very decided habits. He recognizes her authority from the first; not her right to rule, but her actual rule; and if this control be well maintained, a gentle, easy, and cheerful habit of obeying cannot fail to follow. The human constitution requires and necessitates it with unfailing certainty. And with this habit well established the moral aspects of obedience will soon form in the mind as it expands, and will strengthen with the increasing strength of years.

Let us suppose two children precisely alike in all respects naturally, and that the moral sense begins to dawn at any given period; but there is this difference in training during the period of infancy—the one was trained to the habit of obeying, and the other to the habit of exercising his own self-will. Now the moral training of both begins, but with this vast difference: in the one case you have an easy, healthful, and cheerful *habit* of obedience and submission to begin with; and in the other, a veteran self-will and stiff neck of forty years' growth, for a child's perverse self-will grows about forty years every twelve months.

But this infantile obedience must be elastic, mild, and prudently adapted to the infantile condition. It must not aim so much to control the child's actions in every thing as to establish an understanding as to where sovereign control resides. Nothing is more easy or more certain in all cases than to establish this understanding, if pursued from the first. Disobedience and self-will at the first are no stronger than a zephyr, but they grow from the very first with surprising rapidity; and with prudent management they need never be much stronger than a zephyr.

This baby-obedience is generally neglected because the parent sees no immediate advantage arising from it. The disobedience and self-will are smart, funny, and mere amusement. The inconsiderate parents vainly suppose they can establish their control, and bring the child to subjection after awhile, when obedience shall become practically useful. No parent ever succeeded in such an undertaking. It is unnatural.

A child, however young, is a complete man, possessing all the elements of the human constitution. A little time for development is all that is necessary to bring them into active exercise. This development begins at once, and proceeds with great rapidity and certainty, and has made large progress long before moral culture can be begun.

The proper improvement of this period of imbecility is of the utmost importance in after-life. It shapes the moral character by mere habit. The tendency to do whatever we are accustomed to do is the most powerful instinct of nature in either man or beast. Cultivate it properly, and you have a good foundation for character. Neglect it, and the loss is irretrievable.

Indeed, it is quite safe to say that we may go a full step higher. Without any pretensions to physiological science beyond what is open to popular information, it may be confidently stated that the formation of character may be, and oftentimes is, partially formed in the womb of the mother. Large thought must be turned in this direction by thinkers. The improvement of society requires it.

How character, moral, mental, or physical, is formed or influenced in the fetal state we do not know, but that it is done we know very well. That external circumstances and influences acting upon the mother during the period of gestation are transferable, and generally, if not always, are more or less transferred to the offspring, there is no doubt among persons of information. Take two somewhat extreme cases, otherwise equal. In the one case the woman, herself of irritable temper, is subjected to disappointment and crosses; misfortune and little acts of injustice press hard upon her; family discords increase and annoy; she is thrown into society below her grade; her eye, and consequently her heart, rest upon dissatisfaction, and her temper is occasionally ruffled into ferment. The other case is different: the woman is kept in a cheerful mood; pleasant company surrounds her; her visitors are persons of equal intelligence with herself; elevated conversation gives her food for thought; agreeable things and agreeable company greet her.

Now, in these cases the laws of nature require and necessitate a vast difference in the structure of character. A hint to the thoughtful is all that is intended here. The subject is susceptible of indefinite elaboration, and its great importance cannot be questioned. The intelligent and thoughtful man can but look forward to an improved social period when an incoming generation will be far better arranged for than the past or the present, not only in the matter of training and educating proper, but in a greatly improved fetal and even embryonic state. Some one said that men were born savages. That might be doubted as a necessity; but if true, we need not long remain so.

On the whole, see the amount of daily and nightly toil, labor, vexation, anxiety, and wear and tear of mind and body undergone in the course of twenty or twenty-five years by the average mother in the effort to keep her children from immediate harm or outrage! This great burden upon human life is a world of immensity! *Now, nine-tenths of this is unnecessary!* It is self-created, self-imposed. It is not only unnecessary as an extra burden on the mother herself, but the very indulgence of it works detriment and life-long evil upon the children which is fearful to contemplate. One-tenth part of all this maternal labor and anxiety will work a far better and vastly more valuable purpose if applied at the proper time, and in the proper way. Read, and you will see it.

CHAPTER V.

HAPPINESS IS ALWAYS THE RESULT OF OBEDIENCE.

IT is exceedingly important that children be kept in a cheerful and happy mood. Unhappy children make an unhappy household. It is cruel to suffer children to fret, chafe, tease, and cry from hour to hour. The humor becomes soured, the feelings rasped, the child is troubled and unhappy. His sorrow is deep and real, though the cause of it may be what we older ones would call a trifle.

Some of the plainest and simplest lessons of life seem hard to learn. *Happiness is the result of obedience.* This principle is world-wide and never-failing. It is more apparent in children than grown people, for the reason that with children all emotions are quick. Feelings come quick and go quick. Results are quickly seen. Three-fourths, if not far more, of all the unhappiness in children is produced by inconsiderate attempts to meet demands that have been repeatedly denied, and are perhaps impracticable. Children are human persons, subject to human laws. The drunkard tries to satisfy his thrist by drinking, the covetous man by getting, the debauchee by indulgence; and how do they succeed? They add fuel to the flame, and constantly increase the trouble they so vainly try to abate.

A cross, unhappy child—always a disobedient one—already made miserable by indulgence—wants, or imagines he wants, a dozen things in quick succession, each one forbidden in turn, or previously known to be prohibited, and each is after awhile grudgingly or partially granted. And the foolish parent vainly supposes that the fortieth indulgence will satisfy. Such parental wrongs and injuries are criminal. And the complaint is, O what a bad child! It is the natural and certain result of your own doing. Who expects to sow thistles and gather grapes?

God gave you a good child, and you, by your criminal ignorance and incompetency, have well-nigh ruined him. Most assuredly the child is to blame, as much so as you suppose, but you are ten times more to blame. The only way possible by which children can be made happy is by making them obedient; and the only way by which they can be made obedient is to keep them happy. Happiness and

Happiness the Result of Obedience. 43

obedience are twin and inseparable the world over.

Children's wants, mostly whimsical and imaginary, alternately denied and granted, over and over again, in succession and confusion, do but increase the want and the vexation more and more, and wretchedness, vexation, and strengthened disobedience, are the never-failing result.

And this nursery of mischief and unhappiness is far from being the worst of it. It is in these young years that character for life is formed. The temper is soured; angry feelings are engendered, and a spirit of dissatisfaction and complaining becomes fixed; and these follow the man or the woman to the end of threescore and ten years. Traits of character thus become constitutional and changeless. All the quarreling and fighting in the land, with all the sad consequences thereof, all family discord and trouble, with its endless harvest of evils, had their seed sown by thoughtless parents, or was permitted by them, back yonder in the nursery. What fearful responsibility! The idea of ready, unhesitating obedience was never taught the child, and how is he expected to feel its force? And when he comes to learn and know about it, how *can* he feel and apply its force? He has from the first, in early infancy, been taught to *be pleased*, to be humored in his whims, to have his own way, to govern every one around him more or less, and if required occasionally to submit at all in any thing, he has always understood that to do so was a great hardship and wrong to himself. Cheerful submission is a thing he never heard of. To please him is, in his estimation, the great business of life. Then what can be looked for under such training?

And at the same time nothing is more practicable or much easier than the establishment and permanent continuance of a well-understood doctrine that children are subordinate—that the parent rules, not occasionally and by chance, in fits of bad humor, but permanently and regularly. Then you have a good, solid foundation. You have a settled habit to assist you in governing. There is no strife or contention in the premises. But let the young yearling will rise to the surface, and hoist its tiny banner a few times, and now you have trouble, lightly as you may think of it.

It is a hard thing to inculcate obedience to God and humble submission to his will in children who have not been in the constant habit of submissive obedience to their parents. But with a spirit and habit of *obedience* to any rightful authority once established, the rest follows easily, and without friction.

CHAPTER VI.

COMMON PARENTAL CRUELTIES.

THE heading of this chapter would seem to be harsh language, but it is fully justified by abundant facts. It would not do, I suppose, to say in plain words that crimes are habitually taught in most families, and yet I do not know that the truth would suffer much by such a declaration. There is scarcely a crime in the Decalogue, save one, of which children are not capable, that is not frequently inculcated in its principles, at least, in most families. The foundation is laid, the seed is sown, the principles are inculcated.

Anger, resentment, quarreling, fighting, and murder, are only different phases and degrees of the same crime. All crimes are taught in their rudiments first—thoughtlessly it may be, but none the less certainly for that. Anger is the immediate fruit of disobedience, and resentment, hitting back, in fun or in earnest—it matters not much which—is sowing the seeds of fighting and murder.

Early impressions are frequently inculcated

in lessons like this: "Now, George, don't let that boy impose upon you; give him as good as he sends." And then the foolish parents think they are very unfortunate in after-years to find their boy the author or subject of a homicide, and the family in deep distress thereby.

Lying is the parent of more crime than almost any other one thing, and the extent to which this is encouraged and virtually taught is appalling. A mother frequently tells her children fifty lies a day, and in most cases the child knows they are lies. And so in the child's estimation lying is a mere harmless pastime. Children are amused, flattered, threatened, and frightened with forty hobgoblin lies until it is well-nigh impossible for them to have serious regard for truth. "George, I will certainly whip you well if you do not go this instant." But George has heard such meaningless falsehoods too often to be frightened by one now. His wagon needs attention, and his whip-lash has a knot in it; and so he goes, if at all, when more at leisure. "O Susan, you are the very worst girl I ever did see in my life!" But Susan very well knows there is not a word of truth in it, for only an hour ago her father told her she was a very nice girl, and her mother has also told her the same thing frequently. The hiding of Tommy's marbles, telling him you don't know where they are, may be child's-play, but it is germinal stealing, and lying to hide it. If such seed ripens at all, as it is likely to do, its fruit may be looked for in legitimate places such as criminality, the court-room, or penitentiary; or if not in these places, at least in a bad character.

The pernicious influence of thoughtless visitors and nurses in families is still worse. The man is only playing with little Henry, two or three years old, and yet he is systematically planting the seeds of bloodshed and misery to ripen in after-years. Follow these lessons legitimately, and you lodge in the criminal court, or some such a place. The criminal or worthless character of to-day was back yonder the fond little play-boy of a doting mother, whose friend or nurse planted the seeds of this present distress.

The most effectual lessons in disobedience, self-will, and family distress, are often administered in family visiting, which at the time is regarded mere child's-play. That which is jest to the man is a serious lesson in practical life to the little prattling boy.

A child knows and practices what he is taught. Beyond this the instincts of nature control him, and often lead him to ruin. How can it be expected that a child will submit to control if frequently suffered to have his own way when questions of control arise? What is sinful life but self-gratification? It is not the doing of this or that specifically, but the following of one's self-will rather than yielding to rightful authority. Who has discovered, and where did the information come from, that proper Christian cross-bearing was less useful, less applicable, less necessary, or less practicable, in the cradle and nursery than in maturer years? The laws of nature or of grace are not to be reversed to suit either the ignorance or the whims of either parents or children. Cross-bearing no more interferes with the proper flow and enjoyment of life in children than in those of maturer years.

CHAPTER VII.

TOO LATE, TOO LATE.

WHAT a world of complaint we have about bad children! The world seems full of bad children. And yet whatever bad children there may be were made so by their parents. God makes no bad children. And now the hypercritic interpreters of Solomon and Paul are distressed, lest our children should be regarded as something above or different from so many masses of moral putridity and corruption. Still I will insist that God makes no bad children—parents do it. God makes nothing bad. The moral state of young children will be looked at after awhile. At the present it may suffice to say to parents that God gave you good children, and gave you directions how to train them; but by negligence and thoughtlessness of duty you suffered them to follow their natural instincts, go astray, and so they very early became very bad. One says, "O how I have tried, and labored, and prayed, to make my boy obedient! I am fully aware of the necessity, but have not been able; I am sure I have done my best."

Yes, my dear woman, you have labored enough with that one boy to suffice for the successful training of twenty or fifty just such boys. One-twentieth part, and far less, of this labor and anxiety, applied at the proper time, would have made him a docile, cheerful, obedient child, always delighted to meet his mother's wishes, and obey her commands. You began too late—too late, entirely too late. He was a hardened veteran in disobedience, long practiced and expert, at two years old, and that was about as early as you began seriously to think of controlling him. At the first, when God placed him in your control, he was scarcely disobedient at all. A one-musquito-power engine would have turned him in any direction; but at two or three years, a forty-horse-power engine is not sufficient. You sat still and saw the demon grow, until now it is quite beyond any force you can apply. Nature's time to begin was a long ways past before you began.

Labor amounts to nothing, anxiety and care amount to nothing, prayer amounts to nothing, unless timely and wisely applied. A cup of water rightly applied would have arrested the fire at the beginning, but now the engines cannot do it. Half the labor of the world, and far more, is useless, because of untimely and unwise application.

"Just see how Bettie struck Harry in the eye! She has almost put his eye out; and O I have tried so much to break her of that wretched temper!" But, madam, you began too late. She will never be cured until she goes into her grave. She is destined irretrievably to a sour, harsh, disagreeable temper, that will more or less annoy her neighbors and friends through life. Should she live to become a mother of a family, she will most likely bequeath a disagreeable, unamiable temper to her children. But she herself, come what may, is greatly and hopelessly injured for life. Female amiability is forever lost to her. False glosses may cover up her deformities considerably; pride of appearance, as she nears and enters womanhood, will come largely to her assistance. She may succeed somewhat, as most other women do, in hiding her real character from public view, and living a life of falsehood, but true womanhood she can never reach. The disobedient anger was not arrested in its early risings in the cradle; the habit is set, and nothing earthly can break its force. Divine grace may soften it more or less, pride and shame may smooth the outside a little, but the time for cure is past.

"Well, I expect my children are about like those of other people; and I know I try as much as any one can, and it is just impossible to make children obedient."

You are entirely correct. It is impossible if the work is to be begun and conducted as you tried to do it. You governed your children ten times more than there was any necessity for, but it availed nothing because you began too late. You did not begin at the first.

Willie is seven years old. A more cheerful, happy, and contented child I have not known. Since a year old he has scarcely, if at all, been known to cry aloud, except, perhaps, for an instant, on getting hurt, or some such cause. Nature did no more for him than for ordinary children, and very little labor has ever been expended on him to make him obedient, but that little was employed mostly before he was six months or a year old, with a little attention afterward. He knows little or nothing about persistent disobedience. In his childish heedlessness he sometimes requires to be spoken to a second time, but he never obeys with lagging reluctance. Obedience is his habit; he never learned any thing else; his habit of doing as he was told was a settled matter long before he knew there was any other way. If his play and thoughtless inattention betrays him into something probably forbidden, it gives pain, and he lights up with sparkling gladness on learning it was not forbidden. He is never afraid of punishment, for he was never punished.

A child accustomed to obedience regulates all his wants accordingly. His wants are contingent on leave being given. He is accustomed to believe that his parents know best. It is the disobedience that is slavish, irksome, and hard to bear. Crying children were made so by the mother. This rule is never-failing: no child will cry after a year old or so, and keep it up several minutes at a time, except as the result of shameful neglect on the part of the parents. Even if hurt pretty badly, he will cringe and whimper a little; but to keep up a cry, cry for five or ten minutes, or longer, is certain evidence of gross negligence on the part of the parents. But after the habit of crying for every disagreeable trifle becomes established, it is impracticable to stop it except by cruelly beating the child into a slavish submission which degrades and humiliates him so that he never, or scarcely ever, fully forgets it.

All the low-toned, cross, and ill-tempered men and women were made so in the training.

Sick children don't cry any more than well ones if properly taught from the first.

It is very unreasonable to suppose, as most people do, that young children must needs cry and fret a great deal in sickness. Unruly and ungovernable children, accustomed to be controlled only by coaxing, threatening, and hire, will of course carry out their accustomed habit in sickness. A crying, fretting, teasing child, already self-harassed into a fever, "is very unwell to-day, poor child!" and the mother considers "quite unwell" a sufficient reason for a day full of distress to both child and household. Disobedient children sometimes get sick, and then trouble is on hand. The proper administration of medicine is impossible. "A sick child must be indulged," it is said: "how can a sick child be controlled?" Alas! your sick child cannot be controlled, and so he must suffer on. There is no remedy. But a child accustomed to obedience is as readily and cheerfully obedient in sickness as in health.

CHAPTER VIII.

CHILDREN MUST BE BROKEN.

From all I can learn on this subject, I conclude that children from the cradle to adult years are very much what their parents prepare them to be. This rule will admit of a little flexibility, but not much. Habits are made up of thousands of little actions which form themselves into settled customs, which compose what we call character. Children are born with very little character; but character is formed at a much earlier period than many suppose. It is generally very much, if not in most cases, unchangeably shaped in the third or fourth year, if not earlier. Of course, it has not much strength in those early periods, but it is formed, and set a-going.

It is not true that children are born bad; neither is it true that they are born good. They are almost a moral blank, or negative, or innocent. He never committed crime, nor even meditated it. He is born with one single misfortune, or inheritance, call it what you may, and that is latent at first, though it begins to develop at a very early period. This latent inheritance is *self-will*, a stiff neck, unwillingness to submit to authority outside himself. It is not disobedience, but a spirit or tendency thereto. The child is not personally corrupt, but has an innate and certain tendency to corruption. He is not a sinner, but has an innate tendency that way, which we call nature, or natural corruption.

Now, this spirit of self-will, independence, or disobedience, must be removed before such person can become a true man or woman. It cannot be removed by mere outside moral culture. It is not flexible, and will not bend. Nature forbids it. It must be *broken*. We sometimes speak of breaking a horse—he needs no breaking; he requires only training. Neither would man need any thing but training if, like the horse, he were to remain in the infantile or imbecile state.

The young child knows nothing of a law of God; his parents are his lawgivers. But this loyalty soon begins to transfer to the Almighty. Now, if this self-will be thoroughly broken in the imbecile state, when it is so easily broken, then we have a conquered, subdued, obedient child to enter upon the responsibilities of life, instead of one with a refractory, unsubdued spirit.

Let this great practical lesson be well learned and acted on, and society shall rise octave after octave, and childhood-life shall be of tenfold more value to mankind.

But here we meet two classes of objections: the one is from the mother who "raised ten children," and knows this to be impossible. She has tried it faithfully, and knows, etc.

The truth is, she knows nothing about it. She gave birth to these "ten children," and supplied some of their physical wants, but she never "raised" any. They grew up around her as willfully disobedient as she herself did, and as the bent and tendency of uncircumcised and unsanctified nature requires. These mothers who know so much scarcely ever saw an instance of true obedience in their lives. A broken self-will in the cradle, leading to cheerful obedience, maintained by the constant care of a pious, intelligent mother, ministering nicely and naturally to the earliest and simplest religious lessons, are matters never dreamed of in their philosophy. These children of whom these mothers know so much were all hopelessly ruined, without a miracle of mercy, as they themselves were, before their "raising" began.

The next objection is from superficial-thinking Christian teachers. They do not see how there can be personal Christianity unless by a conversion following some years at least of wicked life.

It is very certain that conversion, or regeneration, call it what you may, must always begin a religious life. But I do not see the necessity of waiting five, ten, or twenty years for the conversion, or of waiting at all. Why not make the most direct effort at conversion at the first? Is not the Christian religion perfectly adapted to the condition of man in all ages and in all circumstances? Then what do we wait for? And yet look at our practice! What efforts do we make for early conversion? None! I look over the entire field of pastoral theology, ministerial, domestic, social, and literary, and I repeat the answer to this vital question of early conversion, and I declare that in the course of my life I have not known an effort made, large or small, for the conversion of young children. I never heard the subject alluded to in the pulpit, even in the most general way; nor did I ever read it in a book except the Bible—there I read it abundantly. Nor do I remember to have heard a minister, or man, or woman, allude to the subject in conversation except in the most general way. The only religious teaching and preaching I know any thing about relates exclusively to persons who have lived, at the very least, five or ten years in open sinful life! Indeed, it is well known that very nearly all our ministerial and literary effort applies to the reclamation of persons who have lived in sin twenty years and upward.

We have practically settled down upon the doctrine that ten or twenty years of sinful life is a condition precedent to religion. I do not believe that willful disobedience, continued at all, a day, a week, or ten years, is useful at all, but is bad, and that continually, and bad for every thing. Sin, much or little, is bad, and wholly bad. A conversion at ten years is much better than no conversion at all; but that same case would have led to a better life, other things equal, if the conversion had taken place eight or nine years earlier. And yet I have heard, by Christian ministers, congratulatory remarks on "early conversion" at ten or fifteen years! Conversion breaks the stubborn self-will, and religious life keeps it subdued.

CHAPTER IX.

OBEDIENCE IS NOT SLAVISH.

IT was Selkirk who said, "I am monarch of all I survey." So far from obedience being slavish, it is the only thing that does, or can, produce the largest liberty. There is nothing good, either in individual or social life, that is not the product of obedience to rightful authority, nor nothing bad that does not grow out of disobedience. Obedience is the foundation of loveliness in children, of womanliness and manliness in youth, of amiability in maturer life, and Christian excellence in all. It is the only constitutional distinction between right and wrong, between high character and low character. Disobedience is the prime, approximate, immediate, remote, and efficient cause of all evil in persons and society. It causes all the troubles in the family and out of the family. It produces all crime, fills all prisons, most of the early graves, and causes all the distress of mankind. Right and wrong, happiness and unhappiness, freedom and slavishness, are but other names for obedience and disobedience.

The notion that obedience restricts liberty in young or old, is the climax of folly. Look at mankind anywhere, and you will find that it is the disobedient, and he alone, that is deprived of liberty. It is the disobedient child alone who is treated slavishly, and governed almost beyond endurance, while the obedient one only is governed but little, and is free, cheerful, and happy. The more a child is disobedient, the more he is governed, a hundred to one, and the more he is curbed, restrained, hampered, and restricted in his wants.

Just in proportion as a child's self-will rises, his imaginary wants increase, his whims become extravagant, until a trifle is magnified into great anxiety and irritation; instead of parental control, there has been no little parental contention, with alternate success and defeat, and in the end the child has undergone an amount of control, loss of liberty, real or imaginary wrong, and felt degradation greater in one hour of strife, than an obedient child would experience in a life-time.

Two children want to ride. In the one case the mother says, "No, Mattie, you can't go; you must stay at home and play with sister." Mattie submits instantly, is not at all discomfited, the disappointment is slight, and soon forgotten. In the other case, Kate is told the same thing, but she has not the least notion of giving up the contest. Two or three successive demands and denials produce a cry of resentment and determination to resist encroachments upon personal rights. Appeals for sympathy and protests against wrongs soon bring father and big sister into the strife. "What shall I do with the child?" exclaims the mother. "You are not dressed, and how can you go? There is not room for many in the carriage." And then changing the base of defense, in softened tone, "Well, darling, never mind now; Charles shall get you a nice new carriage, and nice white horses, and shall ride you and sister away, away." But baby has heard such lies before to her heart's content, and kicks and cries the harder. At length the child either succeeds by a clear and open victory, giving sure promise of success in the next battle, or if the denial be urgent, the poor girl is imprisoned by force like a criminal, and in distress no little she feels outraged and determined to be more successful in the next battle.

Now, in these two cases the disobedient child has been *governed*, her liberty restricted, and her wants and comfort abridged, a hundred-fold more than the other. Obedient children—that is, those taught obedience from the first—are governed very little; they need but little. Obedience is a habit. They have confidence; or if more strictly theological language be preferred, they have *faith* in their parents, and submit lovingly and cheerfully. Those children who have been suffered to indulge a bad temper, and they alone, indulge in seasons of hatred toward their parents. They feel wronged and injured, and most assuredly they have been well-nigh ruined.

At dinner-time Sally sees some company in the house, and whispers to mamma, "Will there be room for me?" "No, my child, you must wait." And Sally is off in the bed-room amusing herself without a murmur. But in another similar case the crying, the threatening, the false promises, increase the restraint until the real hard pressure of iron force and cruel control, operating upon the tender, inexperienced constitution, amounts to real distress in no small measure.

It is both unjust and cruel to throw the blame on the child, and say he deserves it all. Certainly he is a bad boy—she is a girl of bad habits; but the parent, not the child, is the great wrong-doer. The parent stood by and saw the bad habit rise from that which would not outweigh a feather, and grow and strengthen, and did not put forth a finger to restrain it, and the child could not do it. A very little well-directed effort back yonder would have saved all this sea of trouble, as well as the life-long degradation that is to follow.

Children should be governed as children, not as prisoners or captives; nor, on the other hand, as dolls and playthings. They should have the largest liberty. Don't attempt to put old heads on young shoulders — they won't grow. Let the boys go—and girls too—and romp, and play, and make a noise, and break things, if need be. Things are made to be broken, and throats are made for noise. But all this must be inside the strictest obedience. There is plenty of noise for romp and play, but none for anger; and there are plenty of things to be broken by accident, and helter-skelter, but none for spite and self-will.

It is an invariable rule that children are happy, and feel free, just in proportion as they are taught to be obedient, and those who enjoy the largest liberty are the least governed and most submissive. Children generally suffer a hundred-fold more government than is necessary. An ounce of government in the cradle is worth a ton out of it.

But no woman can govern children until she first learns to *govern herself*. Fretting, scolding, complaining, and threatening, on the part of a mother, will ruin any children. They never can make the men or women they would otherwise.

CHAPTER X.

THOUGHTLESS TRAINING.

THE child who is not required to obey, and take on a regular habit of obedience as a settled principle of life, is wronged by his parents out of his dearest and most valuable rights. The foolish neglect of many parents at this point is criminal. Disobedience, or reluctant obedience, which is the same thing, is inculcated almost scientifically, as if it were the intention. The child is told by his mother every day, in various forms of expression, that he will have his own way, that she cannot control him. He is threatened with punishment fifty times a day, but such talk is mere idle words in the child's estimation. Children are imitative, and when they hear their parents tell things frequently which they know to be untrue they are sure to follow the example.

Baby-talk, continued after the early dawn of the period when the child can discern articulate words, is less criminal than telling falsehoods, but it is a great disadvantage among children. A child can understand language very well long before he can utter a word. It is, then, very important that children hear words pronounced correctly in order that they may imitate them properly. Children accustomed to hear words mumbled, or half-pronounced, or with baby-pronunciation, will mumble and mispronounce their words likely through life.

Putting children to sleep is a tax on household labors of no small extent. The one or two hours' labor of each day is but a small part of it. The cross and ill humor, and peevish, fretful disposition it engenders, is a much larger item. The habit is never excusable. Almost the smallest amount of patience and common sense will easily establish the regular custom in any child of going to sleep when laid down for that purpose. And it is just as easy to establish the custom of rocking, or walking or rocking, a child to sleep. Any well-handled child a few months old will always go to sleep in two minutes when told to do so. But children who form their own habits haphazard, generally require to be put to sleep at a cost of no little time, trouble, and vexation.

Although there is great difference in the natural disposition of children, some more or less inclined to this or that trait of character, yet they are all alike in this one thing—they are all easily susceptible of forming habits. Accustom children to any thing possible, and they tend with almost irresistible strength to that thing. Indeed, what is oftentimes regarded as a natural trait of character is nothing more than a habit early formed. No natural characteristic, however distinct and specific it may be, is at the first stronger than a zephyr. Its strength is acquired by habit invariably.

Parents generally bring up their children about as they themselves were brought up. Here lies the difficulty. But it must be overcome. Parents must learn the necessity of cradle-government. It must be enforced by all the means at our command.

Extreme indiscretion is very frequently seen in parents and others talking about children—relating their exploits or their delinquencies in their presence. The one tends rapidly and strongly to excite pride and fanciful dreams of greatness, and puff up with wild notions of superiority, while the other tends to depress laudable feelings, and make the child feel mean and degraded, and to rate himself below his superiors. If a little girl hear it said that she is a very bad girl, or the worst girl in the neighborhood, she must either feel degraded or believe the person saying so tells a falsehood, though it be her father or mother. The child of two years is listening attentively to every word uttered in his hearing about him.

But of all the wrongs and disadvantages children are subject to at the hands of the mother, a fretful, scolding, or threatening treatment is the most damaging. The children of a woman who cannot patiently govern herself must suffer on through life. Quit, O quit threatening, scolding, and complaining! Be patient. Fathers are almost always too loose and indulgent, or too rigid. A boy or girl of six years and tolerably developed mind has feelings, and expects them to be respected. A harsh denunciation or coarse threat of punishment is not soon forgotten by a child of tone and high mind. Such treatment tends to brutalize the feelings and corrupt the manners.

CHAPTER XI.

WHIPPING CHILDREN.

WHIPPING children with a rod or other instrument of torture is a simple, cruel, unmitigated barbarity. It belongs to darker ages than these. In an enlightened age, and among civilized people, it is a crime that ought to be punished by the civil magistrate.

And on this I suppose the antiquated wiseacres and old-granny philosophers will raise a shout of horror, lest the character of old King Solomon should be underrated; for they revere him as a great child-whipper. And so every child must take his share of the birch and the cudgel, if for no other good reason, to preserve the good character of the great Israelitish king. Solomon may have been a great whipper of children; but if so, he does not seem to have been remarkably successful in the business.

I will not undertake to measure arms with Solomon, nor will I agree to be governed by all his interpreters. If he undertook to change the constitution of nature—which, however, I am not able to see that he did—then I do not admit that he had a right to do so. God made a distinction between men and brutes, and even brutes would not need to be governed with a club if the law of governmental kindness, obedience, and control, were well enforced with them from the beginning. I do not know that brutes would need club-government if they were taken in hand at the beginning, and governed properly.

That children are very frequently — nay, very generally—found in a condition where the whip is a necessity is very certain; and it is for this necessity that the parent needs and deserves the punishment I prescribe for them. The child created the necessity without knowing it: the parents—with their eyes open, and whose special duty it was to prevent it, and when it might be easily prevented—stood by with folded arms and saw this necessity grow from a germ as light as a feather to the strength of half a hurricane. The parent may accuse Nature, but Nature hurls back the complaint in thunder-tones. Any half-fool parents can read, if they have no eyes to see, that the child is in constant tendency to evil and ruin. But what are parents made for, and put here for, but to counteract and prevent the growth of this tendency? None but a sluggard complains that weeds grow; for what are plows, and hoes, and muscle, and health, made for? Does not everybody know that the world, wholesale, would soon become a pandemonium but for man's labor interworking with the grace and mercy of God? That the rod of restraint is often necessary is well known. So are the prison and the gallows. But that does not prove that all men must be hanged, or that everybody should be put in the penitentiary. May not this evil tendency be headed off? May not a habit of obedience be formed despite and in the teeth of this evil tendency? This I understand to be the mission of Christianity and parenthood.

A brute cares for the whip just in proportion to the measure of its sting; but to a human person, young or old, it degrades, blunts, and brutalizes the feelings, benumbs the sensibilities, and greatly wounds the ennobling and healthful feelings of proper self-esteem. The child may see he had done wrong, but he will reluctantly, if at all, forgive the hand that inflicted the blows.

Punishment of this sort restrains bad conduct only from a motive as bad as the conduct which it is intended to prevent. It is the restraint of fear, producing mortification and debasement in a child as does the pillory and prison costume in grown persons. It paralyzes self-respect, and makes the criminal feel his criminality, which tends to low desperation and a don't-care condition of desperation. No child properly trained from the first can ever need the rod. Its need is the direct fruit of parental neglect. It is a fool's answer to plead necessity. The parent created the necessity.

All penal government is at best but a *dernier ressort*, and its application to the cradle or any other part of the family is a miserable subterfuge which at least punishes the wrong person. It is bad enough to brutalize degraded criminals with it where other forms of control cannot be made to answer the purpose of public safety; but to degrade young children to such an ordeal of control is a showing-up of the savage side of life in a manner not flattering to public intelligence. A household where the rod is a factor in family government is an ill-regulated, badly-governed, and unhappy household. And yet the family where the rod has become necessary, and is dispensed with, is in a far worse condition. Children brought up under birch-law, whether in fact with the stripes or in fear of them by threats and constant reminder, grow up with blunted feelings and mean ideas of both themselves and their parents.

A minister once said to me that he knew no other way to control young children but by fear. And so society is degraded, and the Church greatly injured, by the ignorant notion that children must be kept under *fear* in order to obedience! Nothing belonging to animal life, that ever was governed, is so easily governed as children; and yet half the trouble and misfortune of mankind, if not far more, is the almost immediate result of ignorance and carelessness on this subject.

The following from an anonymous writer I commend to the sober reflection of sober-minded men and women:

If it were possible, in any way, to get a statistical summing-up and a tangible presentation of the amount of physical pain inflicted by parents on children under twelve years of age, the most callous-hearted would be surprised and shocked. If it were possible to add to this estimate an accurate and scientific demonstration of the extent to which such pain, by weakening the nervous system, and exhausting its capacity to resist disease, diminishes children's chances for life, the world would stand aghast.

Too little has been said upon this point. The opponents of corporal punishment usually approach the subject either from the sentimental or the moral stand-point. The argument on either of these grounds can be made strong enough, one would suppose, to paralyze every hand lifted to strike a child. But the question of the direct and lasting physical effect of the blows—even of one blow on the delicate tissues of a child's body, on the frail and trembling nerves, on the sensitive organization which is trying under a thousand unfavoring conditions to adjust itself to the hard work of both living and growing—has yet to be properly considered.

Every one knows the sudden sense of insupportable pain, sometimes producing even dizziness and nausea, which follows the accidental hitting of the elbow against a hard substance. It does not need that the blow be very hard to bring involuntary tears to adult eyes. But what is such pain as this in comparison with the pain of a dozen or more quick, tingling blows from a heavy hand on flesh which is, which must be, as much more sensitive than ours as are the souls which dwell in it purer than ours? Add to this physical pain the overwhelming terror which only utter helplessness can feel, and which is the most recognizable quality in the cry of a very young child under whipping; add the instinctive sense of disgrace, of outrage, which often keeps the older child stubborn and still throughout, and you have an amount and an intensity of suffering from which even tried nerves might shrink. Again, who does not know, at least, what woman does not know, that violent weeping, for even a very short time, is quite enough to cause a feeling of languor and depression, of nervous exhaustion for a whole day? Yet it does not seem to occur to mothers that little children must feel this, in proportion to the length of time and violence of this crying, far more than grown people. Who has not often seen a poor child receive, within an hour or two of the first whipping, a second one for some small ebullition

WHIPPING CHILDREN. 77

of nervous irritability which was simply inevitable from its spent and worn condition?

It is safe to say that, in families where whipping is regularly recognized as a punishment, few children under ten years of age have less than one whipping a week. Sometimes they have more, sometimes the whipping is very severe. Thus you have in one short year sixty or seventy occasions on which for a greater or less time, say from one to three hours, the child's nervous system is subjected to a tremendous strain from the effects of terror and physical pain, combined with long crying. Will any physician tell us that this fact is not an element in that child's physical condition at the end of that year? Will any physician dare to say that there may not be in that child's life crises when the issues of life and death will be so equally balanced that the tenth part of the nervous force lost in such fits of crying, and in the endurance of such pain, could turn the scale?

Nature's retributions, like her rewards, are cumulative. Because her sentences against evil works are not executed speedily, therefore the hearts of the sons of men are fully set in them to do evil. But the sentence always is executed, sooner or later, and that inexorably. Your son, O unthinking mothers! may fall by the way in the full prime of his manhood for lack of that strength which his infancy spent in enduring your hasty and severe punishments.

Suppose that such punishment of children had been unheard of till now; suppose that the idea had yesterday been suggested for the first time that by inflicting physical pain on a child's body you might make him recollect certain truths; and suppose that, instead of whipping, a very moderate and harmless degree of pricking with pins, or cutting with knives, or burning with fire, had been suggested—would not fathers and mothers have cried out all over the land at the inhumanity of the idea?

But I think it would not be easy to show in what wise small pricks or cuts are more inhuman than blows, or why lying may not be as legitimately cured by blisters made with a hot coal as by black and blue spots made with a ruler. The principle is the same; and if the principle be right, why not multiply methods? This one suggestion, candidly considered, should be enough to open all parents' eyes to the enormity of whipping. How many a loving mother will, without any thought of cruelty, inflict half-a-dozen quick blows on the little hand of her child, when she could no more take a pin and make the same number of thrusts into the tender flesh than she could bind the baby on a rack! Yet the pin-thrusts would hurt far less, and would probably make a deeper impression on the child's mind.

CHAPTER XII.

A THREATENING GOVERNMENT.

NEXT to whipping government stands a threatening government. This is of the same nature as the former, though it may not have all its follies and iniquities. Civil government is necessarily a threatening government. Penal laws are in the nature of a threat, or *in terrorem*. It is the best mode of governing adult people that jurisconsults have discovered or legislatures have adopted. But it is applicable to grown persons, and not to children, for the following reasons:

The civil magistrate cannot have immediate control of vicious people. He is not always immediately present, with authority and admonition, to prevent and restrain the meditating offender. The would-be criminal is personally free to do, and public law can only threaten beforehand and execute afterward. But this wide separation does not exist between the governor and the governed in the case of parent and child. The parent can exercise immediate control. Again, a penal law is soon forgotten by a child. But in case of such offenses as are called crimes and misdemeanors, the man or woman is supposed to know all about them, and, in premeditating crime, to run the chances of detection and punishment. This is entirely too distant for child-government. He needs admonition forty times a day for the same offense, or class of offenses.

"Now, Sallie, if I catch you with your apron wet this way again to-day I'll whip you well." How long is Sallie going to remember that? Perhaps five minutes or three. Forty dozen things happen before night, not anticipated or taken into the account when this law to prevent the wetting of aprons was enacted and promulgated. Like many other laws, it has encountered so many changes in the habits and customs of mankind that it has long since become obsolete.

A parent in the habit of threatening, threatens forty things an hour, and thirty-nine of them are forgotten before the close of the hour; so they amount to a tirade of meaningless denunciation. Any child with common sense cannot fail to so understand them. He has heard thousands of such laws promulgated, but does not remember to ever have known one specifically executed. In his estimation, it is a mere customary mode of scolding.

Or if, in some rare instances, the boy or girl may attach some seriousness to the threat, it can have but the same moral effect as the whipping would have. It is part and parcel of the whipping government.

This is not the philosophy of child-government. It is adapted to the government of old, shrewd violators of law, who premeditate and arrange for crime. Young children never do this. They act upon an instantaneous impulse, and should therefore be governed by two different principles of control. What are these?

The reader who has somewhat carefully followed me thus far need scarcely be told. The first principle of infantile control is *habit*. Away with fear, and threat, and birch government! They belong to the ignorance and cruelties of dark and savage life. *Habit* is the best word I can find in the language to express the precise idea. It is proverbially "second nature"—so described by Webster in defining the term. Habit is almost equivalent to his *nature*—it is only secondary thereto. One of the easiest things to do with any and all children is to establish a habit—any habit of doing any thing not extremely inconvenient or difficult. It is very little, if, indeed, any more, trouble to establish a habit of obedience than of disobedience. Almost the slightest care, with a little constant attention, will fix the habit, *if taken in time;* but if neglected at the first, and attempted after awhile, it is utterly impracticable.

> A pebble in the streamlet scant
>   Has changed the course of many a river;
> A dew-drop on the baby-plant
>   Has warped the giant oak forever!

It is an ignorant falsehood upon human nature to suppose it at all difficult to change radically and thoroughly all or any of the natural habitudes of life if taken in hand at the first. Kaspar Hauser lived to the years of manhood with *all* the ordinary habits of life thoroughly and radically changed, and it required no more effort or labor than to establish any one mere commonplace habit. Bad habits will set in of themselves without assistance, because nature tends that way. Good habits require a little assistance, but not much.

Habit-government—kind, simple, affectionate habit-government—is the kind adapted to the cradle, the nursery, and the family. It is not true that children, at the first, are the half-monkey and half-brutish kind of creatures they often grow to be in a short time afterward. And it is about as easy as it is common for indolent, cowardly, and incompetent parents to shift their own miserable delinquencies on to their children, and cry out, "O what bad children!"

That children are bad, very bad, uniformly bad, even much worse than they are uniformly esteemed to be, is very readily believed; but that parents are primarily answerable for nine-tenths of this sea of evil, is also as true. They were placed there for the express purpose of changing this natural current tending to these evils of life, and charged to see well to it at the first, when the tiny current barely moves at all; but instead of doing so, they say, "Surely a current so slow and so small can do no harm," and they wait awhile. At one or two years they find the current a little hard to control, and they vainly say, "I will wait till I can reason with him." And by this time both the volume and the momentum have increased to Niagara proportions. And then the cry is, "O what a bad nature!" heaping their own sins and delinquencies on the shoulders of their children.

The government of threatening is a government of debasement and degradation. Children over whom the rod *in terrorem* is exhibited a dozen times a day are degraded and debased in their estimation. "You deserve a good thrashing, you good-for-nothing fellow!" "Go and bring me a good switch here this minute!" "You do that again, Miss, and I will whip you well!"

It is impossible for children to grow up under such miserable government, and reach manhood, or even youthhood, with any sort of proper feelings of respect for either themselves or their parents.

CHAPTER XIII.

HONOR AND MANLINESS IN CHILDREN.

CHILDREN are at a very early age susceptible of a high sense of honor, integrity, and manly bearing. And the importance of cultivating this principle cannot be overestimated. In this two extremes are to be carefully avoided. One of these extremes is foolish pride and self-importance, and the other slavish fear and subservient degradation.

While boys from five years and upward should be taught carefully to estimate and preserve from waste their own trinkets, books, clothing, etc., they should never, until near maturity, be indulged in the ownership of property of value. This custom invests them with high notions of self-importance, and undue, and unmanly, and unbecoming principles.

On the other hand, children should not be degraded into menials, and made to feel that they occupy a half-criminal or low position. Children of all ages should be made to feel that they are the companions, but not equals, of their parents and friends. Obedience being a well-established habit, it is not irksome, dishonorable, or degrading. Being taught that it is right, decorous, and honorable, it is not submitted to, but rather sought for, courted, and esteemed, as a mark of honor and propriety.

Threats, penal fears, a rod in sight or indicated as a means of government, tend to slavishness and feelings of humility and degradation. Government and coercion are very different things.

"Now, if you do that again I'll whip you well. Do you see those two switches laid up there?" It is humanly impossible for that little girl or boy to desist from the forbidden action without feelings of slavish meanness. How different would it be for little Lizzie or George, accustomed to honorable and dignified obedience, to be addressed on this wise: "Now, my child, you know I don't want you to do that." That stimulates George's ambition and self-respect, and his obedience is his delight. To such a mandate Lizzie's little heart responds in cheerfulness; no law is so potent with her as her mother's wishes.

"Harry, if you don't behave yourself I'll tell your father the moment he comes home, and I'll make him stripe you well, you good-for-nothing fellow! You are the worst boy I ever did see." And that unfortunate boy, perhaps nearly as vicious as unfortunate, is compelled to drag out a miserable boyhood under the imbecile and cowardly tyranny of a foolish and miserably incompetent mother. And when Harry gets to be sixteen or eighteen, and finding home disagreeable, seeks companionship in company as bad as himself, and drunkenness and the criminal court fall naturally into line, the ignorant and badly-raised mother considers herself "unfortunate."

How often has that little girl been threatened with the rod, or the palm of punishment, and sometimes the threats executed, because, as she has been a hundred times told, she was "as bad as she could be!" Now, there is no way possible by which that girl can be relieved from the conviction that she is a mean, vicious, and degraded creature, far below the level of her associates, but by believing her mother to be a common liar and slanderer at home.

And for such a girl to grow to womanhood with self-respect and elevated notions of virtue and amiability, is a simple impossibility. Human nature does not admit of it. As she nears maturity, pride comes to her assistance; she tries to cover over her moral deformities as well as she can conveniently: divine grace may do much for her, but high womanhood is beyond her reach forever. This world has natural laws, and they are immutable.

CHAPTER XIV.

THE RELIGIOUS CAPACITY OF CHILDREN.

AND so here comes up the old question of original sin, and its application to young children, with its great variety of real or supposed issues. I will try to simplify them. They arise largely out of ambiguity and looseness of language, and a pertinacious adherence to set phrases and chosen sectarian words.

On the one hand, we have the doctrine that children are born pure, holy, upright, and they learn wickedness, and so become sinners by mere contact and association—that if let alone, and not interfered with by wicked persons, they would grow up religious, and so would need no *r*egeneration.

On the other hand, we have the teaching that children are born sinners, and necessarily grow up sinners, and can only be regenerated after they attain to age sufficient to enable them to understand the Christian system of 'redemption by Christ crucified.

The truth lies between these two extremes. It is very true that vicious association promotes sinfulness greatly. Evil communications corrupt good manners. But it is by no means true that there is a pure stock to begin with. Suppose ten or twenty infant children grow up from birth in exclusive association among themselves—if such a thing were possible—and they never hear an evil word, or see an evil action, except among themselves. Their moral and religious education is strictly negative. What sort of persons would they be? They would grow up as wicked as very wickedness.

Leaving out of the question right here the pure, original state, and fall of man in Adam, when we look at man as he *is*, we see him subject to the same law of fruit, product, or result, as are the lower animals, or even the vegetable kingdom.

Look at any young animal. That individual has given no indication whatever as to what its course and habitudes of life will be; but when we see the race to which it belongs, we anticipate its habitudes unmistakably. If it be a young tiger, though of itself as docile and harmless as a young puppy, our knowledge of its race compels us to conclude that if left to the bent of its nature, though perfectly innocent now, it will grow up cross, blood-thirsty, and ferocious. A young puppy will grow up to bark and behave like other dogs. A young squirrel will, as it grows up, take on the habitudes of other squirrels. And so we speak very understandingly of the harmlessness of the dove, the cunning of the monkey and fox. Ducks will betake themselves immediately to the water, though they never saw it done before. Horses, cows, and all other animals, have their exclusively peculiar modes and habits of life. And so of all animals. And nothing short of a violent, radical, and coercive training, will divert any single individual animal from the natural course pursued by its fellows.

And just so of the vegetable department. When first out of the ground, the individual plant gives no indication whatever as to what it will grow to be. No one can tell whether it will live a year, or a hundred years, and whether it will produce ears of corn, pumpkins, acorns, apples, or oranges. But the moment we discover the race it belongs to, we know unmistakably its natural course of future development.

But *why* this plant always grows a hundred feet high, in a healthy condition, and bears acorns, and that one crawls on the ground, produces water-melons, and dies in six months, we do not know. We say it is the *nature* of these vines to bear grapes, and of that kind of tree to bear apples; we always see them do that way, and that is all we know about it. The cause lies back behind our reach.

And so we expect an eagle, the moment it breaks the shell, and before, as it grows, to fly high, and build in the rocky cliffs; the whippoorwill to fly near the ground, and always build in stumps and logs; the bullock to graze in the meadow, and the mule to be obstinate and contrary. But *why* these things are so we know not. We always see it so, and say, Such is their nature severally. We know no more. If necessary, we could give names to these primary propensions, but that would give us no information about the thing.

And the same general law precisely applies to man. There is *something* primarily in an apple-tree that causes it to bear apples invariably, rather than grapes, or nuts. There is *something* primarily in a dog that makes him kind to his master and cross to strangers. And there is *something* primarily in man that causes him to behave contrary to the principles of love and justice enjoined in the Bible, both toward God and his fellow.

The name of that cause is far less important

than the certainty of the cause itself. Many will dispute about the name; very few will deny the thing. Look at man the world over, and the rule is as invariable as that animals follow their natural instincts: he is disobedient to God and to the laws of kindness and justice toward his fellow. So there is obviously *something* in him that causes this universal depravity. Whether he inherits it from a near or remote ancestry as remote as Adam, or imbibes it from his fellow by association, or from all these sources, though it be supposed to come from the sun that shines, or from the air we breathe, from seminal taint or from primordial taint, the thing is here, and these inquiries relate only to modes and the names of causes, while the fact does not admit of question. Things not debatable are not debated. Things without an apparent cause we call natural. So we call universal sinfulness natural. But while this badness is universal, it is not true that every thing in every man is bad. It is possible for a very wicked man to tell the truth. A sinful man is not, therefore, a fiend.

Now, how does this universal badness apply to young children? and when does it begin to operate?

A tendency to sin is seen from the first; but there is a period—perhaps from six to nine or twelve months or more—of nearly or quite absolute nonage. In that period he is no more capable of sin than is a parrot. A habit of doing may be established in him, but he is no more a sinner than he is a walker or a talker. He is neither, because he has never walked, talked, nor sinned. You might as well call a horse a sinner! Did he do a thing that he *cannot* do? You may say he is in a sinful state—that is, a tendency to sin is in him just as a tendency to bark is in a dog so young that he never barked.

When old enough to be capable of doing wrong he begins to do wrong, just as the crab-apple tree at the natural period begins to produce sour fruit. This is the rule of Nature. But is there no escape from this early product of sour fruit? Are we absolutely shut up to this necessity? If so, then how long *must* this bitter fruit continue to grow? It ought to be changed from bad to good at the very earliest period possible under the laws of divine grace. How long *must* it continue? But we are told that "the blood of Jesus Christ his Son cleanseth us from *all* sin." And this early sin is not only a part of a sinful life, but by far the most important part of it. And is there no remedy for this vitally important part of sin-life? To suppose it impossible for divine grace to reach sin at this or any other period of life, or any other conditions of life, is, it would seem, to rob the Saviour of some of the laurels attributed to him in the Bible.

Does the gospel limp just at this point? or would not a careful examination discover the lameness to be in our superficial way of administering it? Six months of sinful life in, say the second or third year, is more damaging than the same length of sinning at any other period. This is the formative period. And no grace adequate to it? Well, there ought to be; and there *is*. Grace is abundant, and applicable to all cases.

We have got ourselves into the habit of regarding divine grace inapplicable in childhood before the child is capable of understanding theological terms and doctrines, such as pardon, repentance, faith, sin, Christ, forgiveness, etc., whereas a child's creed is very much shorter than all that. It has but two words: being *good*, and being *bad*. To obey is to be good, to disobey is to be bad. He does not know the meaning of the word obedience, but he knows and understands the thing as well as he ever will. And being *obedient* evinces the highest style of saving grace. A child's faith contains very little systematic or dogmatic theology.

The faith and reasoning that is of manhood is not required in a child, but a child's faith is. "Several ability" is the rule. Moral perception of right and wrong does not set in all at once. Its first opening dawn is not perceptible. Its maturity is not far from adult years. In this period of partial responsibility, as it might be called, the person is answerable according to the great law of equity, "several ability." The earliest capability of doing wrong is, of course, very feeble, but such capability at all implies a corresponding capability of doing right, or, in other words, of being religious. Unavoidable sin is a contradiction. But there is no escape from a tendency to sin. This is universal. It is called by various technical names —corruption, inbred sin, born in sin, depravity, etc. But tendency to sin is not crime. Nature is not crime. A young crab-apple tree has done no more sourness than a young rose-bush. I did not make my nature, but am placed here with adequate means to prevent an evil development of it in both myself and my children.

This is the unfortunate state in which we come into the world. The picture could scarcely be overdrawn. Without help we are destined to irretrievable ruin. But, thanks to God in Christ, *help is provided*. And this help does not propose relief from part of the trouble, but from the whole. It does not apply to us, after awhile, in some periods of life, but to the entire life from the womb to the winding-sheet.

A Sunday-school magazine inquires, "Why should not a child become a disciple of Jesus as soon as he can understand that Christ loves him? Who can prescribe the age at which the Spirit of God begins to work in the heart of a child?"

How well a child may "understand" the vicarious nature of the death of Christ might be a difficult question, and be variously understood. A child of two or three years may be told, and so may know, the fact of the Saviour's death, though none of us may understand much about it. How is it ascertained that the Spirit of God *begins* to work in the heart of a child at all at some period along in the course of his life? This restricts the grace of Christ to a period. I think this grace begins with the life itself, long before the child has any sort of understanding about it. There is no graceless period in childhood. Grace is unceasingly continuous in childhood as in youthhood or manhood. We restrict it when we suppose it to "begin" after awhile as the intellect opens.

I know of no natural reason why a child may not feel divine love as early as he is capable of feeling parental love. He is unable to define or understand it. It is a felt satisfaction of being good. This consciousness of doing right and of meeting approval is a very early development, and is what we mean in later years by "enjoying religion." There is nothing in either nature or grace that inhibits its early beginning. Natural depravity appertains no more to cradle-life than to youth or manhood. It is simply universal. The grace of Christ meets it in the cradle precisely as it does in maturer years. There is no more of a necessary sinful period somewhere in the first five or ten years than in later years.

The above extract from the Sunday-school paper strikes the pivot of this question. Can a child be a Christian, in saving alliance with Christ, in high and wide contradistinction from other children who are irreligious and ungodly, at a period before either has reached a state of intellectual growth sufficient for them reasonably to understand the love of God through Christ in a proper theological sense? Or, in other words, does the Spirit of God *begin* to work in the heart of a child *after*, and only after, he has received and is intellectually able to digest the Bible teaching that Christ died for sinners, and will love and save him on condition of his faith and obedience? Does the Spirit of God *begin* to work in the heart of a child at some period in the course of his life? or is it continuous from the first? Suppose a child to be carefully and piously taught full, submissive obedience to the only authority he is capable of recognizing, and that in trying to be good he maintains such obedience in good faith. How far does that fall short of Bible piety?

What is the religious condition during the space of at least a few years after he is first capable of sin, and therefore capable of Christianity, and before he is capable of theological religion? By theological religion is meant an intellectual comprehension of Christ's merciful work. During these years he is committing sin, and—no place for repentance? No; the gospel is suited to his condition also. Why not?

CHAPTER XV.

THE RELIGIOUS CAPACITY OF CHILDREN—CONTINUED.

AT how young a period are children personally capable of true, genuine, saving faith? This is an important question, and a point that is generally greatly overlooked. The question might be answered in this way: Children are capable of religion as soon as they are capable of doing wrong; or, as soon as they are capable of discerning between right and wrong; or, a capability of committing sin implies a capability of religion.

The period of moral imbecility has heretofore been alluded to. It begins at birth, and continues probably, in many if not in most cases, six months or a year, perhaps longer—may be two years or more. In this period the child knows nothing of right and wrong. I have spoken of it as absolute nonage. In this period he is incapable of religion, properly so called. The grace of Christ applies to him spontaneously, or passively, on his part.

But as the moral sense begins to dawn, re-

Religious Capacity of Children. 101

ligious responsibility begins to attach; and they increase in precise proportion to each other. Along at the first they are both exceedingly feeble. Where little is given little is required. Passive grace withdraws gradually, very gradually, as a sense of moral responsibility increases, and does not depart entirely until both the intellect and moral sense assume their adult condition.

So, in this respect, there are three moral periods in human life: first, the period of absolute nonage; second, of partial nonage; and third, of full personal responsibility.

It is clear, therefore, that the period of personal religion—that is, personal religious obligation—begins with the period of partial moral sense—the second period, as above described. This is, of course, the period when sin is first possible, and, of course, the time when the Christian life proper ought to commence.

But how frequently—nay, I might say, how uniformly—do we fail to even attempt to inculcate Christianity at this tender period of life! The child of two, three, or four years, is generally treated as utterly incapable of religion, as much so as a brute animal.

There are no outward signs or indications that I know of by which we are able to test the existence of conversion with certainty at a very early period. Perhaps the age of about three years, or may be four or six, is about as early as certain evidence of genuine Christian faith or conversion is seen in a favorable condition of things. But then we must not fail to remember that children are capable of knowledge, of feeling, and of emotion, and of penitence, long before they are capable of expressing such experiences either by words or any other certain indications.

It is an axiom, or a truism, and therefore is not to be questioned, that at the very day or hour, if it could be identified, that the child is first capable of doing wrong, he is fully capable of genuine conversion. And if conversion be delayed, it is the same kind of lengthening out an irreligious life as that which occurs at twenty or forty, but with this difference: early procrastination is worse and more deadly than later. This, I say, is a truism, because a child capable of doing wrong is for that reason capable of doing right. Ability to sin, or do wrong, means ability to be religious, or do right. Religion is doing right; sin is doing wrong.

O the miserable evils of depending solely upon camp-meetings and "revivals" for conversion! While I would not underrate them,

I would declare my belief that the nursery, properly used, possesses tenfold the converting means of all the former put together. Hunting up sinners out of the nursery, however positively valuable it may be, is but a mere *dernier ressort*, or last effort, to gather up neglected and squandered opportunities. Most children of religious families, or at least many of them, were converted in the nursery, and their religious state was neglected afterward. Most of the people we preach to are backsliders.

By proper training a child ought to grow up a converted Christian, and not be able to remember to have been otherwise. This doctrine is as old as the Bible. But how far this may be practicable in each or any particular case is another question. That will depend upon the piety and other qualifications of the parents and pastor, and the social surroundings of the child. Here lie the great hinderances, and not in the capacity of the child for early Christianity. It is said of the great and good Richard Baxter that he became much troubled because he could not recollect when he was converted. But he saw that home-education and nursery training were as properly means of converting grace as the preaching at church, and thenceforward contented himself with the sweeter reflection that he had learned to love God early.

It is a great mistake that a child cannot be converted until he can talk about it approvingly and theologically. The conversion of a child leaves him a child still. His is not the conversion of a person of years, with the reflection of long habitual sins piled high upon him. And yet there are not two kinds of conversion; but there are a thousand kinds of experience and sensible effects of conversion. By what rule of infantile development or psychological science can we look for the same immediate effects of conversion in a child of three or four years and a veteran sinner of forty?

To question the practicability of such early conversions involves the necessity of ascertaining how much sin or how long a sinful life must be pursued *in order to conversion!* And the objector must explain the principle upon which sin is *a condition precedent* to a religious life!

Many persons seem to think, and often really believe, that religion does not pertain to children until they are nearly grown; that the most that need be done is to teach them good behavior, send them to Sunday-school when eight or nine, and hope that in some revival they may be induced to repent and be converted by the time they are twenty. This hope is generally realized in perhaps one case in twenty or forty. It is as humiliating to know as it is disgraceful to the Church that it may be known, that this is the general drift of thinking and feeling on the subject even amongst professedly religious people.

And yet they are all in favor of early conversion. O yes, they say, let us have early conversions. But what they mean by *early* is from about fourteen to twenty. It is true, disgraceful as it may be to the religious press, religious authors, ministers and people, that the belief in the Churches in the practicability of substantial Christianity among children from three to eight years, is by no means general, or even uniform, much less is it universal. It is, therefore, not by any means uniform, even in my own Church, which I honestly believe is a little ahead of all others in this respect, that practical efforts are made by pastors and parents for the conversion of our children before the age of about twelve years.

Great honor to the Church and glory to God for the truly great and wonderful Sunday-school enterprise which has so suddenly and so grandly sprung up amongst us in the last half-century! It is at once the glory and wonder of the age how we are beginning to have some little attention paid to early piety. When suitable teachers can be had, conversions among the scholars are sometimes and in some places occasional, and in some few cases somewhat frequent; but it has not been my good fortune to have learned that many of these were under the age of ten years or thereabouts.

It was my misfortune in early life to have known but little about Churches or their work, but for over fifty years past I have been somewhat conversant with both; and it is with deep feelings of pain and mortification that I write, and only because I feel it a duty to do so, in order to call, if it may be, some attention to the subject—that in my experience in the period above named I have heard, I suppose, about the average amount of preaching, have read some religious books, and some religious newspapers, and other periodicals; I have even heard bishops preach; but to-day I am not able to remember where the high duty and great advantage of inculcating early piety—intelligible piety, and conversion at about the earliest practicable period—strongly urged, elaborately explained, and lengthily and laboriously enforced. I have occasionally seen the subject glanced at in very general terms—entirely general—have often seen the Saviour's words quoted, "Suffer the little children to come unto me," etc., but uniformly without adequate comment and enforcement, if any at all. I have conversed with a number of preachers on the subject, and have not met one who did not fully believe in the practicability of the full and proper conversion of pretty well instructed children, with favorable surroundings, of three years old; but I did not hear him urge it, or perhaps allude to it, in the pulpit, nor strongly impress it upon parents and little ones at home.

For these delinquencies, if I am correct in so considering them, I am, in good faith, and I trust with some degree of humility and confession, willing to take my full share. It is only in the last ten or fifteen years that I have begun to wake up to the importance of the subject; and my judgment admonishes me that even now I am but half awake.

I have recently read a book of several hundred pages on this general subject, by an author of no mean repute, and which I see pronounced one of the best on the subject. In this book I remember but a single sentence, briefly dispatched, that distinctly alludes to the practicability of child-training from the first, or of religion in children under eight or ten years, as I presume the author would have his readers understand.

But while I have met during life with so little of *teaching* and *inculcation* of early piety, I have met with no little of metaphysical controversy, even to surfeiting, on such technical questions touching the moral state of new-born infants as this: whether "born in sin," or "born corrupt," or "born under the wrath of God," is the most orthodox expression to denote the exact attitude of Christ toward such children at their birth. The mere metaphysical philosophy of this relation may, or may not, be of some practical use in the Church— I will not undertake to determine. I think it lies rather beyond the domain of pastoral theology. And whether the exact rules of definition, as used by biblical and Eastern theologians, can at this day be precisely determined, may, or may not, be more or less useful. I leave that and similar theories to others. My undertaking is discharged with practical explanations of children's religious duty and high-born franchises under the Christian system.

CHAPTER XVI.

CHILDHOOD IS NATURAL AND NORMAL.

CHILDHOOD being natural, normal, and proper, and the grace of Christ being exactly and equally adapted to all men of all ages, it is as well suited to children even back to the day of birth—or before, I suppose—as to persons of any other age.

Many persons seem to have the idea that children are not susceptible of personal Christianity until they arrive at such age as to enable them to comprehend to some considerable extent the philosophical system of vicarious atonement for sin, and the mode and manner of its application, etc. This is generally impracticable even in somewhat precocious children before about the age of eight or ten years. Generally, it is impracticable before fourteen or fifteen. This will leave children under these ages and over one or two years in a very abnormal condition. They are in this period fully capable of moral and immoral conduct—subjects of moral government—and so they ought to be religious; and yet practically, if not theoretically, they are generally left out of the pale of experimental Christianity.

Here let it be repeated and insisted, that any person of any age—one year or forty—who is capable of doing wrong, is capable of doing right. Capability of violating a law necessarily implies capability of keeping it. Ability to sin implies ability to be religious—not to be partially religious, but to be wholly so. It is not wrong, nor sinful, nor punishable, to be born into and live in this world, notwithstanding all we have inherited from Adam or from anybody else. Nothing is punishable but known, willful transgression, unatoned for and unrepented of.

But there is a constitutional disparity between childhood and manhood which must be, and therefore is, taken account of in all the Divine administration toward men. Children, as compared with adult persons, are thoughtless, careless, improvident, forgetful, negligent, without forecast, and devoid of sound judgment; and along with these are also playfulness, imbecile talking, lightness, and frivolity, momentary excitements, sudden elevations and depressions of spirits, sudden bursts of gladness and of sorrows, with impatience,

CHILDHOOD NATURAL AND NORMAL. 111

and a thousand kinds of seeming irregularity of life and conduct.

These things, being natural and constitutional, are not sinful. Why children are made devoid of the sobrieties of age we may not know; we only see it is so. But being so, and that being a part of the constitution of nature, the constitution of grace adapts itself to the system, and so embraces childhood with all its peculiarities, as well as manhood with its soberer and more sedate ones. And so the gospel is as well adapted to childhood as to manhood.

Hence it follows that the letter of the law of the gospel is seemingly violated, or non-observed, a thousand times by children, when its spirit and meaning, as applied to them, are not in the least infringed. A child knows, and can know, but little of scriptural or philosophical rules. I insist that Christianity is as well adapted to childhood, even from the womb, with all its frivolities and thoughtlessness, as to any other age or class of persons.

Children die; they die at all ages, from one day to twenty years; and, in my judgment, it would be a very defective system of religion that would ignore their circumstances and condition. The Author of children is the Author of religion; therefore let religion *from the first* be the rule of life—the common Christian understanding—and not religion from the years of sixteen or twenty.

On this point Archbishop Whately has some good remarks:

"Whenever a child is capable — which is generally at a very early age—of comprehending what prayer is, there must be some mode of expressing a prayer which will be intelligible to him: let this expression be adopted; let him employ the form which he can best understand, and which may be subsequently modified and enlarged as his understanding advances. No doubt a prayer thus adapted to the capacity of a child must be childish: how can any natural, fervent, hearty devotions of a *child* be otherwise than childish? Is it any disparagement to the devotions of grown men that they are *human*, and not angelic?

"Men who are philosophically religious without devotion or godliness are generally very fearful of the introduction of superstition into devotional thoughts and exercise. Religion, with them, to be valuable or genuine, must be intelligent, erudite, cultured, and philosophical.

"*This* is, itself, the worst and most damaging form of religious superstition. By such a rule, rigidly enforced, it might not be very easy to graduate into Christianity. While superstition, in a dangerous or damaging form, should be eradicated, as far as practicable, in persons of mature understanding or somewhat intelligent, in children and ignorant people superstition is not only not disadvantageous, it is indispensable."

CHAPTER XVII.

THE HIGH PARENTAL RELATION.

THERE is a high sacredness, and at least a *quasi* divinity, in the parental relation, which is seldom appreciated by fathers and mothers. A child enters a new world. His mode of existence is thoroughly and radically changed. Of his infantile thoughts we know but little; they are probably few, and rationally nearly unreasoning. He is a worshiper from the first. Like other people, he has learned as much of God and Nature, and of men and things, as his observations and teachings admit of. He looks for a deity, and finds it first in his mother, and then his father. His nurse and other attendants, however kind and attentive to his wants, never rise higher than ministers of mercy. His parents are his god, and he soon distinguishes them as such above all others. In the possible absence of the father he worships his mother. He recognizes their unlimited authority and their actions as the infallible rule of right. They are divine, and he is human.

And the God of heaven recognizes and sanctions this relation, for he made it, and upholds it—that is, the child's understanding and appreciation of the relation. This, therefore, is good and true religion in its application to all persons in that early period of life. Nevertheless, God himself looks on parents in the truer light of legates, or vicegerents, of the Almighty. While they are ministers, or priests, of God to the child, standing in the place of God, they are for the child, or in his eyes, the Most High himself.

This is the relation. How long does it continue? And how, and why, and when, does it change, and God himself, in Christ, appear before the eyes of the child?

This state of things, where the parent stands before the child as the deity, because the intellect of the child is not capable of looking beyond to a truer and more proper deity, continues during the period of absolute nonage, as herein before described—that is, during the period of the child's incapability of discerning between right and wrong; and as he begins to learn of a higher and diviner power and authority over him, he gradually and almost imperceptibly transfers his supreme allegiance to the God of heaven through

Christ. But he still holds his parents in this office of priesthood, or vicegerency, its potency lessening and lessening until near mature manhood.

Now, if any man thinks that this is not, or may not be, a correct statement of the case, let him know that there is but one other consideration conceivable or possible, and that is that the office of the parent is to bring the child into the world, and supply his physical wants, like any other animal mother, until the child is capable of supplying them for himself. The latter proposition supposes the child to be a mere animal; the former regards him as a being capable of communion with God. There is no middle ground.

Then, if parents would open their eyes in sober reflection upon their true relation to their children, they will feel a much greater weight of responsibility than most of us do. It is no light matter to stand before immortal beings in the soft, wax-like formative period of their lives, in the character of almost Godhood—to go in and out, and mix and mingle with them in all the ten thousand details of practical every-day life, and be regarded and looked up to by them as a saviour, an exemplar, a model of earthly and heavenly perfection. The parent has almost, and in the proper and just estimation of the child has quite, the functions and prerogatives of the Deity.

I once saw a father walking a few steps in a light snow, leaving his foot-prints very plain, and his little boy of eight years behind him, stretching his tiny legs to place his little feet exactly where his father stepped. Ah, thinks I to the father, how have those tracks been made in the eight years last past! And how are you going to measure them in the ten or twelve years next to come? That drunken, worthless man, these convicts, this young, self-important spendthrift of puffed-up Lilliputian dimensions—and all these are what they are because they could, and therefore did, stretch their little legs to step where their fathers stepped.

And that woman of ungovernable temper, of mischief-making tongue, of dancing, frolicking proclivities,.or worse ones, whose head, where brains ought to be, is filled with pictures of the latest fashions—and all these are what they are because their mothers measured, in silken, embroidered slippers, it may have been, or in plain or rustic shoes, those or similar steps before them. It often seems to me that many—nay, most—parents, in their high offices of fatherhood and motherhood, are almost fools on the face of the earth!

This high relation of parent and child is not merely nominal. Its responsibilities and obligations are direct, personal, and weighty. Delinquency here is more delinquent and blameworthy than in any other affairs of life. To defraud a neighbor of a hundred dollars in a contract is bad enough, but not one-tenth so bad as to set a bad example before your child. The neighbor can perhaps recover; he can make another hundred—the child cannot; his loss, increasing as it goes, follows him to the grave. Defalcation in a business matter is bad enough, but failure in performance here is far worse.

A child held to slack-twisted accountability in the nursery is a slack-twisted man or woman through life. This world has no means of supplying the loss. A child unaccustomed to family worship is the loser thereby all the days of his life. This world has no means of fully supplying the loss. Almost every act of yours, and almost every neglect, tends to plant a permanent item in the character of your children. In their eyes you are immaculate, and your conduct the standard of uprightness.

And it is also true that, while the conduct

and belief of the parent exercises so great an influence over the child, the reciprocal relationships of life are in full vigor and activity, giving the child a silent but powerful influence over the parent. There is something inexpressibly wonderful in the power of religion *seen* and *acted* in others. Argument is combative, and excites and challenges opposition. Sympathy disarms and captivates.

There is a vast amount of natural life and practical truth in the old story of the conversion of the infidel. There have been thousands such. The preacher was very glad, indeed — always had great confidence in the power of gospel truth and reasoning. How successfully Paul reasoned with Felix! He (the preacher) had, he would confess, made special effort in a number of recent sermons to direct the mind of his converted friend rightly, and now would be glad to know which of these arguments had so happily reached him.

"O," said the convert, "my dear sir, you are mistaken. I had always a ready argument for your reasoning. But did you notice those two little girls converted at the altar last night, and their simple, natural conduct under the effect of it? That was it. I had no argument to meet that. This scene did not challenge my logic. It came up on the defenseless side."

There is more skepticism, practical and logical, among us than many of us are aware of. The eloquence and the logic of the doctors have both failed. Now send a religious child—the younger the better, generally. He approaches "on the defenseless side."

Another point of most vital and momentous importance in the culture of children is set forth in Proverbs xxii. 6, a scripture very frequently alluded to and descanted upon in the pulpit and elsewhere, but by no means always well understood: "Train up a child in the way he should go, and when he is old he will not depart from it." The word *train*, as we read it in our language, or *train up*, we are told by the biblical critics, while it will bear the meaning of teaching, persuasion, admonition, etc., administered directly to the child, its primary meaning in the original language is to *dedicate*, or *consecrate*. Dr. Clarke, expounding this text, paraphrases it, "*Dedicate*, therefore, in the first instance, your child to God, and *nurse, teach,* and *discipline* him as God's child, whom he has intrusted to your care." This same word translated *train* is elsewhere rendered *dedicate*. See Deut. xx. 5; 1 Kings viii. 63, and several other places.

This seems most strikingly simple, devotional, natural, and proper. The relation of parent and child is very close. In very young children they almost coïnhere in a single individuality. Their severalty is an after-growth. Judah, in his appeal to Joseph, said that Jacob's "life was bound up in the lad's life." The parent and child are bone of each other's bone, and flesh of each other's flesh. How can a parent fail to dedicate the child to God? How can parents be in Christ, and their children remain out of Christ? By all means let the children be dedicated. The baptismal dedication is a Church affair; the parental dedication is household consecration.

CHAPTER XVIII.

ELIGIBILITY TO CHURCH-MEMBERSHIP.

IN the many treatises afloat on the rearing and government of children, it seems to be an open question when the proper time is to begin to cultivate in them religion proper. All agree that from a very early period, so soon as they are fully capable of distinguishing between right and wrong conduct, they should be taught good behavior, good morals, and the general notion is that this is an excellent mode of preparing them to become religious at the proper future time. But when is the proper time for them to take on, embrace, profess, and enjoy religion?

Moral conduct, in children or grown people, relates to our fellow-creatures; religion goes higher, and relates to God. Now, the question seems to be, When, or about what period, is a child fitted for this higher relation in its amplest forms and highest state?

This is not precisely the question of early Church-membership, about which so much is written of late, though it is very nearly akin to it. It is an absurdity to suppose a person irreligious and honestly in the Church of Christ; and it is another absurdity to prohibit, or prevent, a person—any person—from becoming a member of the Church until he is able to explain and express himself regenerated, or born again, born of the Spirit—or, as many express it, converted—or to know and feel an experience of God's love in his heart, and capable of being explained to the satisfaction of some other person.

Most Baptists do not evidently consider a child or youth capable of religion at all until he shall arrive at such a state of theological knowledge and biblical criticism as to be able to understand at least the fundamental principles of ecclesiastical science, the principles and modes of forming Church-membership, of ministerial authority, and the Christian sacraments. They do not allow him to enter the Church until he understands these subjects as they understand them. Previous to this attainment, he is prepared by moral training for religion and Church-membership at what they call a proper time in the future.

The provision of my Church on this subject —that is, of children's Church-membership— is as follows:

"As soon as they [the children] comprehend the responsibilities involved in a public profession of faith in Christ, and give evidence of a sincere and earnest determination to discharge the same, see that they be recognized as members of the Church agreeably to the provisions of the Discipline."

This direction to pastors must be looked into a little. On page 216 of Discipline, edition of 1875, it is well stated that "All, of every age and station, stand in need of the means of grace which it [the Church] alone supplies." Means of grace, helps to a Christian life, are not to be looked for out of the Church, but in it. This applies to "all, of *every age*." "And it invites all alike to become fellow-citizens with the saints and of the household of God." This invitation as to small children is, of course, made through the parents. But their practical membership in the Church is clearly recognized, for it is in, and not out of, the Church that they are to find the means of grace.

"But as none who have arrived at the years of discretion can remain within its pales, or be admitted to its communion, without assuming its obligations, it is my duty to demand," etc.

I am unable to see the strict propriety of

the use of the word *assuming* in the foregoing extract. *Acknowledging* is, I suppose, what is meant. We do not assume moral and religious obligations. They are placed upon us, with all possible force, by imperial authority, without any consent or assumption on our part. Now, we may, as many do, disregard this obligation, and take the consequences, but that does not lessen the obligation; or, we may recognize or acknowledge it, and promise to fulfill it, but that does neither create nor increase it.

Therefore, as the Church can have no obligations except moral and religious ones, let us construe the law to mean that we are to *acknowledge* its obligations. This, and then to fulfill them, is all we can do. The pious, well-instructed child has, of course, been doing these two things every day and all the while. It is in these two things that his piety, or obedience, consists. He may, or may not, be able to look back to the period, or about the period, when by divine grace and personal determination he first entered upon this religious life. That is quite unimportant, and would depend mainly upon whether the period would carry his memory far enough back into the dim twilight of childish or infantile experience — a mere historic fact lying upon the surface of life. If he have the experience now, then he has it.

Like older Christians, his religious obligations do by no means rest upon any mere verbal promises he may have made at any particular time, but rather in a felt consciousness of the rightful authority of God over him. His acknowledgment of God's right to govern him, and that he must obey, and delights to obey, has had a hundred-fold more expression in his every-day life and constant pious walk and conduct than it could have in any mere verbal promises.

So here is a class of children which seem to me not well provided for in the above arrangement. Let us explain:

George and Robert are of the same age—say eight, or nine, or fifteen. They were baptized at the same time—in early infancy—and shall here represent two classes of children. George, from his earliest recollection, has been taught to consider himself a member of the Church. His baptism and the obligations of Church-membership have all along been fully explained to him. He knows full well that Robert, and all children of such character and conduct, are not in the Church, though baptized. He sees they are not religious. From about three years old George has given constant and satisfactory evidence of piety, and is always glad he is in the Church, frequently expressing regret that others are not. His pious life is well known to pastor, parents, and others. His general conduct—considering always that he is a child, and not a man—will compare favorably with the average Church-member.

Robert has lived differently. Notoriously out of the Church—never pretended to conform to its rules, or meet its obligations. His baptism was laid aside—practically repudiated. At the age of ten or fifteen he becomes serious, repents, reforms, and joins the Church for the first time.

His case is well met by the above provisions of discipline. But how about George? For him to stand before the Church in a class of persons just now stepping into religion for the first time, and joining the Church for the first time, and promising for the first time to keep the rules of the Church, and abstain from wicked conduct—for George to do this would be a contradiction and a falsification of what he and everybody else knows to be true. He promises, as a primary undertaking, that which is by no means a new undertaking as it is with Robert and the others, but the very things he knows he has been doing from his very earliest recollection. How can *he* join the Church, and at this late day—be it at eight years or eighteen, or any other age—promise, as for the first time, to do what he does not remember ever to have failed to do?

George has been for weeks and months trying to exhort and persuade his friend Robert to join the Church, and be religious, and had frequently prayed that God would give him a new heart, and make him a good boy; and now that he has succeeded, he is told that he himself has all the while past been in the same category with Robert, and must, like him, commence a religious life anew, join the Church anew, and begin anew to be religious. This would be as clearly unjust as it is palpably impossible.

I am unable to see a reason why George—I mean children, girls or boys of that class—should be required, *in the course of a well-recognized religious life,* to *assume the obligations* of the Church verbally and categorically any more than any or all the older members.

Now, it so happens that in my own case personally I never was received into full connection in the Church. And have I not, therefore, acknowledged the obligations of the

Church? (*Acknowledge* is a better word here than "assume.") Rather, is it not well known that I have done this every day of my life for a half-century past, however much I may have failed in fulfilling these obligations? Would a thousand verbal promises strengthen the acknowledgment? Would a verbal promise and undertaking to be honest strengthen the obligation among honest men? Nevertheless, I see very plainly in case of a man confessedly dishonest heretofore, and desiring association with honest men, why he should walk squarely up to the altar of justice and promise and undertake.

It may be said that the pastor ought long ago to have "recognized" George as a member of the Church according to the Discipline —that he should have done this as early as the child recognized himself as a member, and actually conformed to the rules. But this was a clear impossibility. At that time it was impossible for George, or any intelligent, well-instructed child, to respond intelligibly and in good faith to the questions propounded in the Book of Discipline. The language of the Discipline is far beyond his years and understanding. Of many of the terms employed a child of three to five years can have no clear understanding. Under favorable circumstances this would require the learning of twelve or fifteen years. Simple as this language is to men of information, it sometimes requires mature years, or nearly so, to comprehend it all fully.

There is this, however, that might be done, but it would not be perhaps quite "according to the Discipline": The pastor could talk with a pious child of three, or five, or six years, and in simple child's language ascertain if such were really the case that the child knew that Jesus died for him and for all good people—that he was glad it was so—that he intended to be good, and do every thing the Saviour wanted him to do—to mind papa and mamma—that he intended to say his prayers every time, and learn his lessons, and that he wanted to be in the Church. This is reasonable, natural, practicable, and philosophical. It meets the case before us fully. But you require him to answer promptly and categorically that he will renounce the devil and all his works. He cannot do it. He does not know what *renounce* means; he never heard the word before. He does not know that the devil has any *works* by that name; he never saw them, and does not know how they look. He does not know that the world has any *vain pomp,* or *glory.* He has often heard the word glory, but always supposed it meant something wonderfully good, or heavenly. "Vain pomp" the child knows nothing about—never heard the words before—does not know whether it is good or bad, or how it would look if he should see it. He knows what it is to be good, but never heard of "ratify" before.

Indeed, these entire questions, propounded to a pious child, might as well be written and read in Arabic, Hebrew, or Choctaw. A little boy or girl of five years does not comprehend an idea in them. Nobody ever could suppose that they were either calculated, or intended, for small children. They are exclusively for grown people, or very intelligent persons nearly grown. Here it might be said, Let the parent, or pastor, teach the child beforehand the meaning of these terms. But this is the very thing that is impossible. A smart, well-instructed child of eight or ten might, perhaps, be taught the mere literal meaning of the words, but his acquaintance with the world and its general sinful character is very far insufficient for him to comprehend their practical import. So I am not certain that our Discipline in this particular place "*recognizes*" that entire class of Christians represented by George, though it provides well for Robert and his class.

I hope nobody will intimate that this class is too small to be particularly provided for. That would be disgraceful. This class of pious Christian boys and girls certainly ought to be one of the largest, most promising, and interesting, in the Church. Let parents and pastors do their duty, or even some goodly portion of it, and this can never fail to be the case.

So may it not be well that we strongly recommend and encourage the full and proper Church-membership of pious children on the ground of their piety and well-lived and unrepudiated baptism, irrespective of such literary knowledge and intellectual attainment as would enable them to give intelligible answers to all these legal and technical phrases of the Discipline? These questions are well put where they are applicable; but what about the few cases that are, and the millions that ought to be, where they are not applicable?

Why not look for and work for high Christianity among the babes and sucklings of three, or five, or six years, or younger still, where the Saviour said it was and ought to be? Might not a few additional words along here in the

Discipline make better provision for young, pious children?

The Discipline, as it now is, is not applicable to pious, religiously-reared children. It does not seem to suppose there are any such; and may be this is one reason why there are so few. The Discipline provides for the return of such children as have gone astray, and kept astray, in outward wickedness for ten or twenty years or more. They can return, as a very few do, and acknowledge their baptismal vow. But where is the provision, rational and apparent to the child himself, for piously-reared children—those brought up in the nurture and admonition of the Lord?

CHAPTER XIX.

WHAT IS THE AGE OF RELIGIOUS CAPABILITY?

THE constitution of human nature forbids a categorical answer to this question, and yet we can state some things, axiomatic and otherwise, which will go far toward an elucidation of it.

1. It is an axiom that cannot be questioned, or too often repeated, that any person, young or old, who is capable of doing wrong, is capable of doing right. The one necessarily implies the other. Religion is doing right—irreligion is doing wrong. Sin is the transgression of the law—conscious transgression. It is the same, therefore, to inquire how early in life is a child capable of doing wrong—any thing wrong—as to inquire how early he is eligible to Christianity. The two periods are necessarily one and the same period.

2. No specific, namable amount of religious, theological, or ecclesiastical information, or attainment in knowledge, is necessary to the fullest and highest enjoyment of religious peace, love, and obedience, in all circumstances of life.

3. We generally ascertain the inward state of persons by what they say or profess; but we cannot do this with small children. Children *know* far beyond what they are able to *tell*. They have neither the mechanical nor literary use of language, nor the practice of arranging words to tell their feelings or thoughts. They have ideas, as clear and distinct as they ever can have, several years ahead of their ability to describe them orally. We do the child, therefore, great injustice—we are liable to do it—when we subject him to such an examination about his religion as we would an older person. Our technical phrases are all Greek to him. Ask him about God's love in his heart: he does not know that he has a heart, only as he knows that he has a liver. Ask him if God for Christ's sake has forgiven his sins; and he does not know what Christ's *sake* is. You must ascertain his religious state by other means than a dictionary and a grammar. We do not depend upon mere language and literary examinations in getting into the feelings of a child in other matters, and why should we in religion? The child has learned the meaning of but very few words, and they are nursery-words. He knows the use of food as well as the wisest, but he does not know the

use of a stomach, or that there is such a thing as digestion. He knows that God is all about the house, and can see him all the time, and will take him to heaven, and that heaven is just above the tops of the trees. A very smart and eminently pious child supposed the stars were holes in the sky through which God looked down upon us all. Astronomy might find some fault with that idea, but religion could not.

A physician called to see a sick child would be regarded as deficient who would turn away because the patient could not answer questions clearly that would form the structure for a diagnosis. And yet he has the same means, and better, of discovering the physical state of the child that the minister has of ascertaining the spiritual state. The direct literary use of words is of but little value in either case. In case of the physician, I can see the need for ascertaining exactly the inward state; and in case of the minister, I can see a general usefulness in his being acquainted as well as may be with all his people; but I am unable to see, and certainly I have never seen stated, any necessity for an exact spiritual diagnosis in order to determine whether the child might or might not be received into the Church. I don't know what practical use the minister would make of the information if he could get it. The child is rightly in the Church, whatever may be his age—in the absence of persistent wickedness, or determined repudiation of Christianity, which is, I suppose, about the same thing.

In the Church is a better place to cure and improve his bad conduct than out of it. That he is a proper candidate for the highest Christianity is not to be questioned. The Bible, as well as the early Church, is full of children's religion everywhere from Genesis to Revelation, and from Abel to John. It is staple in the practice of the prophets, and fresh in the teachings of Jesus. The child's place is in the Church. Religion out of the Church is not only an error, it is more; it is an absurdity, because it is a contradiction. If a child behave badly in the Church, teach him better. Encourage and admonish him. He cannot be considered incorrigible. That can be supposed only of grown people, or those nearly adult. Proper treatment will plant solid, fruitful Christianity in the heart and life of any child. The wickedness of the world, be it much or little, is the fruit of bad early training.

At the time of the writing and insertion of this particular paragraph I chance to be in Washington City, and have attended some of the revival-meetings of a noted evangelist, in which has been produced a very great work of grace among children, mostly from about five or six years and upward. At one of these children's meetings, there being perhaps twenty ministers on the platform, a Presbyterian clergyman of more than three-score years, from Philadelphia, I believe, in a short address, in congratulating the Churches on this gracious work among the children, remarked about as follows: "Now since it is but a very short time [perhaps he said a year or two] since we first regarded it possible for children to be religious, what may we not look for in the future, seeing that so many are brought to Christ here in these few days?" I was surprised at the declaration, and hoped that some of us might be excused from that category. And yet, practically, will not this strange blunder have a fearfully wide application?

This minister seemed to labor under the strange idea—popular as it may be—that children, or youths, rather, must know so much, must attain to such and such degrees of theological learning, before they can possess the grace of everlasting life; whereas the rule is, "He that believeth hath everlasting life." How old must a child be in order to *believe what you tell him?* Who will say a smart child of two or three years may not *believe* as well as one of twenty? When intellectually capable of believing, he is required to believe, we may well suppose; before that time, he is saved without it.

But how much God requires of small children is a question that must be referred to each particular one. Like older persons, they are accountable according to several ability. But if my child were to die at four or six years of age, when all the sermons and obituaries say he is safe, I would much prefer that he be practically and intelligibly pious than ignorant of God and Christ.

CHAPTER XX.

EARLY IDEAS OF RELIGION.

THE great cardinal and fundamental ideas of religion are as clear, distinct, well formed, and true in well-taught children of three or five years as in doctors of theology of three-score and ten. Religion has very few necessary ideas; and children have but very few ideas. A child of two or three years, or more, has just two ideas about religion and morals. They are fundamental, and really they comprehend all the ideas I know any thing about on those subjects. A child comprehends perfectly well what it is to *be good* and to *be bad*. These two things he understands perfectly well. It is right to do right; it is wrong to do wrong. He ought to do right; he must not do wrong. This is his creed; this is his religion; this is his system of morals.

And does any man's morals, any man's religion, rise higher or go beyond that? Does Christianity require or recommend any thing higher or more than that? Certainly not. The theologian, or Christian moralist, may divide and classify these fundamental principles, and teach separate parts severally and separately, while the child cannot; but human ingenuity cannot, and revelation does not, go beyond the simplest child's creed—to be *good*, and be *bad*. There is the acme of human perfectibility assisted and accompanied by all the grace known to human salvation; and there is all the depth of ruin and damnation known to the curses of Scripture revelation. The man who lives beneath the sun, of any age between the womb and the grave, in any conditions and circumstances of life, who *does right*, is a Christian of the highest type. Did divine grace ever assist to do more?

But it may be said that Christianity implies divine grace in the heart, the transforming work of the Holy Ghost, in addition to the doing of the man. Of course it does; that is to say, doing right implies two things: first, the utmost of human effort; and secondly, the inward work of the Holy Ghost. There can be no doing right without both these things. If man could do right—fulfill the measure of divine requirement—without the assisting grace of God in Christ, then I see no necessity for Christian atonement. It might be useful, but could not be necessary. The person, old or young—surely it matters not what age—who does right, or, in the child's language, is "good," not only has, but feels, the grace of God moving him to such conduct. But the feebleness and inaccuracy of language are such, even in grown people, when employed to describe spiritual things, that in the attempt one will use these words, and another those—very feeble at best, and quite unsatisfactory to both speaker and hearer. And in case of a child who cannot even describe a horse by his general color, how can you expect him to describe an inward, spiritual emotion?

Let the universally admitted doctrine be stated here that we cannot speak a good word, think a good thought, nor do a good deed, without the grace of God assisting us; and then let us be reminded that sin is as deep, universal, and pervading, as it is generally believed to be by the best and most intelligent Christians; and then we may see the more clearly that all good and right among men is of grace. But will you deny a child a year old a participation in this forgiving, converting, transforming, saving faith and grace, because he is unable to describe it according to your most approved classical formulas?

A child can feel, and appreciate, and deplore

—yea, and can commune with God—as accurately as his father or his pastor, but he has no words with which to express his emotion. The notion that a Christian must be able to express, in approved and acceptable phraseology, his conversion—the time, place, and circumstances of its occurrence—so that other men may judge of its genuineness, may have application, and does have application, to some persons of considerable open experience in outward sinful life; but to apply it to a child of tender years would be to turn the constitution of nature out-of-doors in all its application to infantile life.

A child under five or six years cannot *tell* you much about his religion, because of mechanical and literary reasons—yea, and because of intellectual reasons—but he may *have* religion, the best and of the highest type known to grace and experience. And I suppose it is because of the sublime purity and high evangelical character of the religion of "little children"—as it may be, and therefore ought to be—that it is so highly recommended to grown people by the Saviour.

What religion did the Saviour esteem most and recommend highest? Not the religion of theology, nor of Church-science,—not the religion of doctrines, nor of history, nor of literature; but the religion of little children.

Outward actions are not religion, properly or legally speaking; they are rather the evidences, or manifestations, of the existence of religion. Intelligent adult persons can give information, as in other matters of feeling and inward impression, by words and comparisons; children cannot. Moreover, with children, as with all uninformed persons, much more importance is attached to outward forms than with grown-up, intelligent persons. A child attaches great solemnity and importance to forms, and attitude, and posture, in prayer and other religious exercises. Set times and forms and exactness in devotion make a great impression on the infantile mind. These should be encouraged; they make impressions which, if cultivated and kept alive, will tend largely to the building and establishment of a sound religious character, and to blunt the edge and weaken the force of many temptations in maturer life.

The more didactic teaching of abstract principles, to be interwoven into practical life, is useful for persons accustomed to thought and reflection, but not for children who are almost thoughtless. In them you must inculcate thoughts more by words and outward actions. Forms, and attitudes, and examples, impress children. Bible incidents of early piety, and other incidents, stimulate emulation. They are far more easily impressed by constant repetition of simple nursery prayers, Bible verses, and Scripture facts, than by didactic religious instruction. Modes of teaching must be brought down to a child's capacity. You cannot talk intelligibly to young children about conversion, and God's grace, humility, and the like. Their sphere of intellectual knowledge is small. Children are as child-like in matters of religion as in matters of property, civil government, jurisprudence, and other branches of philosophy.

A child's worship consists in acts, and not much in sentiment and pleasurable emotion. He will go to the altar to be prayed for if you tell him, and if he sees others do so, and will feel a degree of satisfaction in doing so, as he would in saying his evening prayer without missing many of the words; but it is naturally impossible that he can feel the humiliation, the resignation, the heavy sense of guilt and forgiveness, of an old and intelligent sinner. You may say his condition in the sight of God as an unregenerate sinner is the same.

This is true only in a strictly legal sense; practically it is not. God regards him as a child-sinner with but very little sinful life and experience, while he looks upon the other as an old, experienced veteran in transgression. Nor can a child regard himself as what he is not. *He is not conscious of a life of defiant wickedness and rebellion he has not lived.*

Tell him to give God his heart, to throw himself entirely upon the atoning merits of Christ, and such like technical and figurative language—these words are all Greek to him, he understands very little about them; but tell him Jesus died to save him, and keep him alive, and make him good,—that he lives in heaven, and loves all good children, and will take them to heaven when they die if they be good, and that he must be good—this he can understand.

The great practical instrumentality in religion is prayer; and surely no prayer rises to a higher plane of either natural or divine requirement than that of a child. Prayer is not estimated in heaven by the style of rhetoric, the measure of its literature, nor by the choice or pronunciation of its words, but by the earnestness and simplicity of reliance with which it is uttered. Then there can be no prayer more potent or more effectual than that of a child. Rightly taught, he looks to God for help with as much direct and immediate confidence as to his mother. It may be said his prayers embody and set forth but very little intelligence and solid thought of God and eternal things. They may be characterized as hasty, and flippant, and devoid of much consideration. Be it so. That is all true. He is yet a child, and not a mature man. Not only his prayers, but he himself, in every characteristic he possesses, is of little solid thought and intelligence about God, or any thing else. He is hasty, flippant, and devoid of much consideration about any thing. But the important question is, Is not Christianity as well adapted to *that state* of life as to any other? In the frame-work of Christianity, so to speak, was not the cradle, and the nursery with its known flippancy and lack of sober consideration, fully considered and provided for?

Repentance, too, is a vital ingredient in Christianity. And it may be said of a child that his sorrow for sin is very superficial. Of course it is. The child himself is superficial. In every aspect you will view him—moral, mental, social, and physical—he is all superficial. Nothing about him has any deep foundation.

And is he expected to be less natural, less himself, in his religion than in his other developments?

It is children we are talking about—prattling, inconsiderate, flippant, shallow, and thoughtless children. When they become men and women, they are likely to put away childish things, but not before; and they will then put them away not because they are wrong, for they are not wrong. They are as right and as useful as the most sapient thinking of three-score and ten years. And is not Christianity as well and as exactly adapted to the young, however young, as to the old, however old? Who will question it? It is no greater an error, nor no greater an absurdity, to suppose some people too old to be religious than that some are too young. They are *never* too young. If alive, they are always at the right age.

CHAPTER XXI.

IS SIN EVER NECESSARY?

I SUPPOSE every man will say it would be both contradictory and absurd to presume that sin was, or could ever be, necessary. Well then, if we settle that as an inviolable principle, and do not forget it as we pass along in this review of children's religion, it will give us great advancement, and save us a great deal of argument. *Sin is never necessary.* Sin may, and should, *always* be avoided. Whenever an act of sin, of whatever grade or character, is committed, or by whomsoever committed, it must be said the thing ought not to have been done; the improper thought ought not to have been thought; the wish ought not to have been wished; the feeling ought not to have been indulged; the act ought not to have been done; but in the room and stead of the improper thought, wish, feeling, or act, religious, pious, holy things should and might have been done.

In other and shorter words, a person—no matter about the years or circumstances—any human person, capable of doing wrong, is capable of doing right. If capable of sin he is capable of religion. It was said back yonder that obedience—full and complete obedience to rightful authority—was religion in its highest signification, and that all sin was but disobedience. Now we are told that very young children commit sin sometimes. They go astray even from the womb. So do men go astray from their attainment of majority. So they are, of course, at each period capable of religion. A child, therefore, capable of doing wrong, of disobedience in much or little, is then and there capable of the highest type of religion; and so is a man, at any age. So we have reached an important point. A child so soon as he emerges from his early infancy—which I have designated his absolute nonage, in which he is intellectually incapable of a moral action at all—is then and there capable of the highest type of Christian perfectibility. We reach this conclusion not only by the demonstrations of logical reasoning, but we have Scripture proof and illustration also, and abundant.

We read in Scripture that "the wicked are estranged from the womb; they go astray as soon as they be born, speaking lies." But this and any similar declarations do by no means imply that there is any more likelihood or aptitude for sinfulness at or near the earlier than the later periods of life. Indeed, the reverse is the case, because sin produces greater and greater aptitude to sin as it progresses. Scripture predicates sinfulness of the whole man; no more of early childhood than later years. The difference is, the later the more difficult its removal.

So we have settled an important point in Christian theology, a matter that has jostled the minds of many. Many persons have lived and worshiped, and some, it is feared, have preached, under the belief that a part of every life must be spent in sin. This is very lofty Calvinism. The regenerating grace of God does not *need* sinful conduct, much or little, as a basis of operation. Cannot grace regenerate from a sinful state as well as from a sinful life? All are in a sinful state; but some do not live long enough to enter into a sinful life. If sin can be cured it can be prevented.

But how far this or that parent could reduce these principles to practice, in the present state of the Church and the world, and in his particular neighborhood, is another question. And if one could, under extremely favorable conditions, it does not follow that another could. Some parents are miserably incompetent just here. If *good* training cannot be quite reached, it can be partially reached. Great improvement is certainly within the reach of all; though even this will not be reached except by those who reach after it.

How can "babes and sucklings" render proper and profitable praise to God but by pious obedience and inward holiness wrought by the Holy Ghost? And the Saviour himself said that we must all of us receive the kingdom of God "as a little child;" not as a man of years, understanding, and erudition, but rather as a little child. Go, therefore, to a child, a little child—and not to a doctor of theology—for example and instruction in the higher faith and experience of Christianity. Examples of infantile piety are by no means wanting in Scripture.

And when we look at the simple, confiding, unhesitating faith of a child, before the subtilties, sophistries, and ingenious lies and practices of maturer years have warped his understanding, we see some of the finest specimens of human faith known to the Christian character. A well-taught child has no more doubt or hesitation about God's protecting care of "good" children, and that he will take them to heaven when they die, than of his own personal being. He believes it with the highest Christian faith.

Is there any better or higher religion than this? The Bible calls it the highest and best. It may be said the child is unacquainted with the distinctions and relation of the triunity of the Godhead; that he understands very little about the time, place, reasons, and character of the crucifixion of Christ; and, in short, that he is almost wholly unacquainted with the various doctrines of Christianity. This is very true. Names, history, biography, doctrines, biblical literature, etc., pertain to Christian theology, to the philosophy of religion; but the simple, comprehensive faith of Christianity—that which brings God and salvation into the soul—does not necessarily include any particular amount of learning in regard to any or all of these things. It does not necessarily require more of intellectual learning than what relates to being *good*.

No person can be a Christian—one year old or forty—without his intellectual knowledge being well-seasoned with revealed godliness up to, or according to, his capabilities. The child of two years or less comes up to this requisition, and the theologian of three-score years, with his diploma, does not rise above it. God, either in nature or grace, does not put old heads on young shoulders. Christianity adapts itself as well and as fully to the child whose entire system of morals and religion is comprehended in the simple idea of *being good* as to the maturer man. If the latter can answer promptly the exact difference between regeneration and adoption, it is because of his superior intellectual culture, and not because of his stronger faith in God. No man has stronger or better faith than a child.

I repeat and insist upon, and again repeat, the great and self-evident truth that a child, however young, capable of doing wrong is capable of doing right; if capable of sin, he is capable of holiness; if capable of disobedience, he is capable of obedience; and if capable of being religious, he ought, then and there, to be solidly religious. To deny this would be to affirm that sin is sometimes necessary.

I repeat and insist upon this point because of its vital importance, and because I see around me among parents and pastors such an indisposition to recognize religion in children, or even to make direct effort to plant it there, until they are nine or ten years old or so, and until they see and understand enough of theology to induce them to go to the altar to be prayed for, or perform some such act, and then describe their feelings in approved language. I would not have religion recognized or fancied where it is not—alas that there is so little among our children!—but I would have right efforts made to plant and inculcate it in the early nursery, and then to keep it watered, nurtured, and a-growing.

A very great and important object is secured, and easily secured—O how easily!—by merely training a small child to do something habitually, be it ever so trivial, from a sense of religious obligation. Such religious ideas well and early fixed in the mind, if reasonably cultivated, will never leave him. Such acts and beliefs may be said to be superstitions. Of course, they are superstitions. Early piety is necessarily superstitious—that is, it would be superstitious in better-informed persons. Objectionable superstition can be predicated only of persons whose intellect and reasoning powers are sufficiently matured and expanded to be able to carry on a process of induction, and who willfully or negligently fail to do so. Superstition, so far from being objectionable in childhood-thought, is naturally inherent in it. Children think superstitiously about every thing else, and why attempt to exclude it from matters of religion? Without superstition, there could be no mental childhood. It belongs necessarily to the early openings of the mind, and is laid aside only as the reasoning faculties mature.

CHAPTER XXII.

THE FICKLENESS OF CHILDHOOD.

THE differences between children and older persons in sobriety, calculating thoughtfulness, firmness of purpose, and stability of character, are well known; but to suppose this natural fickleness and instability is any impediment to a child's religious faith, beyond the seductions and temptations common to man, or to suppose it an insurmountable barrier, would be to impeach the Almighty either in his system of nature or of grace. To the full extent and alongside of such a supposition must lie the absurdity of supposing a period in early life—of eight or nine years, or, at least, of some years between the dawn of conscious knowledge of right and wrong and the ability to study Christianity as a science, in at least its doctrinal rudiments—when he is neither an outcast from God nor a proper subject of faith and grace.

Childhood is natural. With all its careless, heedless, forgetful instability of character; with all its playful trifling, its butterfly eagerness for momentary and changing excitements, its high and rapid hilarity one moment, and its overwhelming, tiny grief and disappointment the next; yea, and its constant and instantaneous exposure to momentary temptations and aberrations—in all these, childhood is natural, eminently natural, and philosophical. I know not why it might not be as highly esteemed as an indispensable endowment of our nature as the more grave sobrieties of maturer age.

And is there no saving faith, no regeneration proper, no holy communion with God, no full, high Christianity, for the tottering boy of three years, who values his new painted marble more than his father values his farm? or for the suckling at the breast who has learned to *be good?* Scripture teaches me that God is pleased with the worship of babes and sucklings.

I repeat, I know not why it would not be as wise to suppose that some people might become too old to be religious as that some are too young. Religion is not for some people, but for the race. Intellectual knowledge in those endowed with it and prepared to exercise it—however useful it may be, and however responsible men may be for its use and legitimate exercise—is certainly not a condition of grace or of faith. A child of two years is responsible for the due exercise of the intelligence he possesses, and not for that he does not possess. The grace of Christ recognizes the infancy.

A person late in dotage or early in nonage, or childhood, will be very likely to do, inadvertently, many things that would be inexcusable in persons of vigor of intellect. Children, and all imbeciles, act from the impulses of the instant, and from what they see and hear. The reflective faculties are almost dormant. A pious child whose religious faith is as sound as the soundest requires, for instance, to be admonished half a dozen times before breakfast that it is Sunday; and then, perhaps he has been spinning his top or shooting his marbles half a dozen times. A child of one year is answerable to the condition of a child of one year; and so of two, of three, of ten, and of forty.

But the Christian religion adapts itself *perfectly*, not half way, to the condition and circumstances of *all*—as well and as fully to the one as to the other. This principle can be denied by nothing short of the stupid blasphemies of infant damnation. Passive grace, or salvation, belongs to the child of absolute nonage, and to him only. He has no moral activity. This condition is the result of divine, not human, action. Moral perception begins, though we cannot tell precisely when it begins. There is, and can be, no such thing as a "line of accountability." There is a state of accountability which sets in in childhood at some indiscoverable period, and opens and develops very gradually and almost imperceptibly, and in great variety of degrees of progress, according to a great variety of circumstances; and God deals with us all, children and aged, according to our exact condition and circumstances. Several ability is the rule.

There is as much religion in the rattling, noisy, heedless, helter-skelter romp and hurrah of childhood, always ready to be brought to bay by proper command, as in the Sunday morning's study and preparation for the pulpit by the minister. Both are alike natural, obedient, and philosophical. Each fills the place of divine appointment and designation. God never puts old heads on young shoulders, nor wrong heads on wrong shoulders.

Moral accountability to God is recognized, we would suppose, in about the same period and circumstances as to parents. Does not the discreet mother sometimes see that the child of one or two years, or older, did something wrong knowingly? and surely the Almighty has not less perception. But neither the discreet mother nor the Maker would hold the child of one year answerable to the same straight-edge of responsibility as the one of five, or the child of five to the same degree as the one of fifteen. The existence of moral accountability at all is one thing—the means, modes, and measures of its discharge involve other considerations.

So the discreetness, staid sobriety, and consistency of conduct, required in adult Christians are no more to be looked for in Christians from the cradle to eight or nine years than we should expect such prudence of behavior in persons of that age in other affairs of life. Childhood is not anti-Christian, nor wrong in any respect. God made it.

CHAPTER XXIII.

CHILDREN GROWING UP SINLESS.

ALREADY the reader has been several times, but not too often, reminded that obedience to rightful authority—full, submissive, unhesitating obedience, not mere doing—is the highest style of true religion; not of theology, of course—that is a science—but of religion. Religion is humble, submissive contriteness of spirit *felt* and acted out. It must also be borne in mind that practical Christianity is not only adapted, but perfectly adapted, to all classes, ages, and conditions of humanity where there is any—the least—moral accountability. And it must be remembered too that the dawn of moral perception—we all being born in a depraved state—implies the necessity of active obedience in order to saving grace and faith.

The question whether a child can be reared without sin must be understood to be practical, and not merely theoretical. And so I reply that it is not susceptible of a categorical answer. It must be first inquired, What child?

To inquire whether it is practicable for some one particular child to be brought up sinless, and whether human nature admits of such a thing at all, under any possible circumstances, are two different things.

And also it must first be understood what is meant by the terms "without sin." Does the question mean a state of absolutely exact holiness? or exemption from such inward tempers and outward actions and words as are cognizable to our dull senses and described in Scripture as sinful? These are believed to be very different things. The former, I suppose, is incompatible with a state of probation. In that sense, no man lives without sin. I suppose our most fervent prayers and best acts of devotion are sinful, and require the constant grace and intercession of Christ to save us from condemnation. Our best righteousness is but miserable rags. "All our righteousnesses are as filthy rags." (Isa. lxiv. 6.) Conversion is not in the nature of a divine diploma. The Christian religion places us all, young and old, in a position or attitude where the forgiving grace of Christ shines full upon us, and is constantly, not occasionally, relieving us from the damning effects of our sinful condition.

The question, therefore, to have a meaning,

must be understood to inquire if a child can be brought up in the absence of such outward acts and the indulgence of such tempers as are forbidden, and are avoidable in ordinary practical Christian life. And the inquiry must relate to some particular child, or to children in some particular circumstances.

A child of irreligious parents, surrounded by bad associations, cannot be brought up without sin, nor indeed without a vast amount of wickedness. The better the instructions and surroundings, the better he may be brought up. We may look into our best families and best neighborhoods, and inquire if this child can be brought up religiously. I think it probable we have some parents so favorably conditioned that this might possibly be done with reasonable satisfaction. It will require much care and watchfulness. And no doubt there are many families where it might be partially done. And that very great improvement in this regard is within the immediate reach of all of us, is very certain. Surrounding wickedness, in either chidlren or grown people, should not deter us from undertaking a deep and wide-spread increase of Christian holiness. And if we cannot accomplish all we would in a day or a year, we must persevere in the right direction, and not be weary in well-doing. From bad local and incidental conditions and previous neglect in our own early years, it might be difficult to find children with whom a religious life is practicable. But what of that?

But surely this does not answer the question as it is intended to be meant. The question meant is, Does human nature admit the possibility, under *any* circumstances that *can* exist, of children being brought up without sin—that is, religious children from the beginning? By religious children I mean religious in the sense that we count the better classes of religious people to be such. I do not inquire for young children absolutely free from blamable indiscretion, for there are no such persons either old or young. If there were any, I cannot see that *they* could have any further need for a Saviour. That question, so explained, I do not consider difficult to answer.

We who live along here in these very early, crude, beginning ages of the world's history have very little idea of an entirely religious neighborhood of any extent. We have none of us ever seen one. Indeed, a whole religious family of any considerable size is very rare. And most of our religious families are—some of them, if not all—more or less indiscreet, negligent, or ignorant as to the very best method of managing children and of directing all their own associations with them. So that children, even the most favored as to religious opportunities, who live in these current ages, as well as those behind us, have, and have had, but miserably poor opportunities for a favorable beginning of a religious life.

But the world is advancing in morals and religion, and consequently, in early as well as late opportunities of religious improvement, Christianity is rising, deepening, spreading, taking deeper and deeper hold on the moral vitals of mankind. If we could see it in a thousand years, and then in ten thousand, and then in a hundred thousand, or in some periods away in what seems to us almost inconceivable or diuturnal ages to come, we should see it much changed. Perhaps the time is not comparatively very distant when the most irreligious neighborhoods of the world will compare favorably with the most religious ones to be found now. We must not be so blind both to Scripture and reason as to doubt the coming of such times. Christianity is going to be a success. Scripture says so, and reason says so. The world—all of it, every inch, to the last son of Adam—is going to be thoroughly, solidly religious to the very core.

Now look at some of the children to live in some coming years or centuries, and see them when from birth they neither see nor hear *any thing*, either from parents or anybody else, but the utterances and breathings of holiness. They are *reared in* the nurture and admonition of the Lord. They are taught, and see all others taught, to worship and *be good* from early cradlehood. So we see that this great question, about which so much is said and so little is understood, needs only to be explained. Then it answers itself. What is practicable in given circumstances, and what is possible with the race in *any* circumstances, are two very different things.

So that, while God does not require impossibilities, or impracticabilities, of any of us, either in regard to children or others, he does require that we regard little children as proper subjects of the highest and most approved Christian faith, and that we teach them accordingly, and not wait for their conversion away along when they get to be five or six or ten or twenty years old. The conversion ought to be in the embryo dawn of the earliest twilight of moral perception, when to human observation it may be imperceptible; and then the child should be *brought up in* that faith. It is not enough that he be brought into it after some years; but that he be brought up in it from the first. The better his instructions and associations, the better and higher will be his religious character.

Jesus did not himself wait until he became ten or twenty years old before he set us an example of life. He was Jesus our Exemplar from the first. We see him first in the manger; and then he passes on through each and every successive day, week, and year, to mature manhood. He was no more our Exemplar in and during any one year, or month, or day of his life than any other year, month, or day. He did not begin his religious life after awhile, but when he began to live. He was as truly and fully Jesus Christ our Saviour in early infancy, playing with his mother's trinkets, or romping in the nursery, as at twelve years talking with the doctors, or later in instructing the Jewish ruler. He was our Jesus all the way, and at every period of the way. While as much of a child as other children, he was never out of the Church nor out of practical Christianity.

CHAPTER XXIV.

LOVING AND FEARING GOD.

AMONG all the instructions, admonitions, illustrations, and examples, touching the subject of early piety in Scripture, either general or particular, there is nowhere the slightest intimation that children are ever too young to be proper subjects of Christ's kingdom. During absolute or infantile nonage, grace with them is passive, or received passively; but its activity begins with its practical responsibility—with the early opening dawn of a consciousness of right and wrong. This is the uniform doctrine of Scripture as well as of reason. Every human person, half a year or half a century old—the principle is the same—is individually responsible for active faith in Christ according to his means of knowing, and considering his social and intellectual circumstances.

Perhaps it never happens that children a year or two old or so, with ordinarily sound minds, are wholly destitute of a sense of moral responsibility. The degrees of strength or feebleness of this sense, and the small number of the things to which he is capable of applying it, are other questions. The existence of the sense at all fixes the personal responsibility; and we can see no way, suggested by either reason or revelation, how this responsibility can be met but by faith in the atonement of Christ. The child does not of course know, and cannot be informed of, the meaning of the word atonement; nor does he literally or historically know any thing about Christ. The germinal principles of all moral and religious action—rectitude, liability, blame and praiseworthiness, etc.—cluster in his almost embryonic intellect in the simple idea of doing or being *good*, or the opposite. That is as far as he has learned in the system of moral and religious philosophy and ethics.

Of course the divine administration recognizes the exceeding attenuant and slender responsibility and moral sense of the little ones. Christianity proper begins—ought to begin—with the very first opening sense of moral responsibility.

Now, what is the duty of parents? It is to bring up, nurture, teach, educate the child, from the first, *in* this admonitory doctrine. Parents are not to prepare the child by moral regimen *for* it after awhile, but to *bring them up in it* from the first. "Train up a child *in* the way he should go," says Scripture, and then, such is the immense power of habit, quickened by the moral sense kept alive, that, as he grows old, or when he grows old, he will not depart from it.

This is the doctrine of Scripture. Infantile religion—proper, sound, heart-felt, devoted religion, but not theological doctrines — is to be inculcated from the first germ of opening moral sense. "They brought unto him little children." They were *little*, probably not old enough to walk, and so were brought. And some said, "O take these babies away; they are not old enough to be religious; teach them to behave well, and when they get old enough to comprehend the responsibilities involved in a public profession of faith in Christ, like this of ours, then bring them." But Jesus taught them a different lesson. They were babies, for "he took them up in his arms." Most likely they were from one to two or three years, or under; and he said to those around him: "You are greatly mistaken, brethren, if you think these children are too young to be religious. Their faith — that which they ought to have if properly taught—is exactly the high, and sound, and acceptable kind that I recommend to the best of you. Their religion — that of which they are capable—is the best and highest kind. This children's religion, and none other, is that which will take a man to heaven. You must not think lightly of little children's religion, for that is the very kind that I recommend to and enjoin upon you all."

We do not know how long the Saviour taught this important doctrine and lesson to the people on the occasion referred to by Matthew and Mark—their synopsis of his teaching is so exceedingly brief—but from all the circumstances, considering the immense importance of the subject, and the numerous times and attitudes in which it is brought so prominently forward, in both the Old and New Testaments, we are justified in supposing that he treated the subject somewhat fully, if not exhaustively. Perhaps he spoke an hour or two, or more. But though we are not informed how long he taught on the subject then, or how frequently or lengthily at other times, we are well informed as to *what* he taught; and that is enough for us to know. He taught that the faith of little children—what it ought to be, and might be—was the highest, and soundest, and best.

He taught that children should be *brought up in* the nurture and admonition of the Lord; that is, as I understand it, in the Church, with its teachings, nurture, and admonition—not to be so brought up as possibly to be brought into this state and condition after awhile. Nature and grace put them into the admonitory Church-state without the agency of pastor and parent beyond due nurture and culture; and now it is the duty of parent and pastor to *keep* the children there, and bring them up in that way.

The duty of parent and pastor is, therefore, to keep and bring up children in that condition and relationship to God in which Christ placed them by birth, and not suffer them to stray out of it. Let them alone, or half train them, suffer them to become disobedient and to grow wicked, and they very soon, and very certainly, wander from the nurture and admonition *in* which Christ says they must be brought up. This teaching looks exceedingly plain. Such children, so brought up, are religious from the first. They no doubt stray every day, if not almost every hour, into many unconscious improprieties, as I suppose all living men do in point of fact, more or less— for no man is absolutely pure or immaculate—

but not into willful disobedience; or, if so, it is quickly repented of.

Another point right here deserves notice. What is this "nurture and admonition of the Lord" in which children are to be brought up? Does it relate to the Church? Is the nurture and admonition of the Lord to be found in the Church, or out of it? I answer, *In the Church*, most assuredly. The Lord has no discipline, no government, no rules of life, no "admonition," outside the Church. Every thing outside the Church is wrong; every thing inside—really and truly inside—is right. There is no right place outside the Church for any thing; there is no right place outside the Church to do any thing. There ought to be no outside. Outside is the devil's territory; inside, and inside alone, is the domain of Christ. The commander of an army does not give orders to those over in the ranks of the enemy, whatever might chance to be the particular views or degree of belligerency of any persons over there. There is but one command given to those outside the Church — that is, Come in. We are not required to improve our condition outside the Church, for we are not allowed to *be* outside at all.

Children are to be brought up in the Church,

not out of it. The admonition *of the Lord* is exclusively inside. The Lord does not work outside except to order men in. "Train up a child in the way he should go, and when he is old he will not depart from it." Train him *in* the way—in the Church, for that is the way in which he should go. The command is not to train him *for* the Church at a future time, but in it. To prepare for entering the Church is nonsense. Now, just as I am, is the rule.

CHAPTER XXV.

CONVERSION, OR NEW BIRTH.

CONVERSION and new birth are generally understood to mean the same thing, though the former implies a turning round or away from a former course of wicked life, and by divine assistance and grace entering upon a religious course. It is understood to imply the new or spiritual birth, or regeneration. But the term is hardly so perceptibly applicable to a person whose religious life begins at so early a period that there has been but little room for, or but little consciousness of, a course of known, practical, sinful life. Regeneration is absolutely necessary in all human persons. Young children have no knowledge of a wicked or sinful *life*. They have not yet learned so much of the world as to know that some people live in sin, and need to be converted. For mere lack of general knowledge they do not understand any thing about conversion, or the necessity of it. They suppose everybody is religious, or rather they do not know what religious is, as contradistinguished from characters irreligious. They look upon their parents and the older children as models of proper conduct; and to follow them, and do as they do, and obey, is, with them, the perfection of uprightness. So they know, and can know, nothing about conversion, in the most proper or technical sense.

I desire to keep as clear as I can from all ambiguity of language, and all subtlety and refinement of criticism, and give the plainest ideas in plainest words, and so, if I can, to smooth or make plain some of the seeming antagonisms along here, where perhaps the difference is more in terms and accepted definitions than in matters of substantial belief.

Children are born into the world in such a state—call it by what name you will—that a *regeneration*, or spiritual birth, or beginning, is absolutely and indispensably necessary. This regeneration is not necessary solely because of something *he* has done, or failed to do, but because of his state, condition, race, nature. A young child is not a sinner, for he never sinned—in the same sense that he is not a walker, for he never walked; is not a talker, because he never talked. He is not even a sleeper, for, as yet, he has never slept; he is not even an eater, having, as yet, not taken food. But because of something, we may not know what—indeed, we *do not* know what—you may call it nature, original sin, inbred corruption, depravity—and these may be more or less correct names of the cause, but are certainly not the cause; but because of something in him, but not created by him, he is as surely, by his bent and inclination, destined to become a sinner as to become a walker, a talker, an eater, or a sleeper. There is *something* in him that causes, and by the uninterrupted course of nature necessitates, this result. Is it because of his guilt? No; of what crime is he guilty? Multiplying synonyms would but darken counsel.

There is a law of nature which we have all seen in its effects, but which none of us know any thing about, or at least do not understand, which applies here just as it applies in both the animal and vegetable kingdoms. Reëxamine a former illustration of this point.

Look at a young animal—any one; take a horse. As yet it has of itself given no indication whatever as to what course or habitudes of life it will pursue; but we see that in all the millions of instances heretofore, young animals of that race have put forth the ordinary behavior of horses, which is strikingly unique and peculiar as to all other animals. He never eats flesh, and lies at the door to bark at and bite the intruder—nor does the dog ever graze in the meadow, and neigh and frolic with the colts; and yet, by viewing any individual dog, when young, and by such knowledge alone, no man could say whether his course of life would be like that of a goat, a bear, or a panther. A young tiger, in every instance, by regular bent of nature, is cross, revengeful, and blood-thirsty; a dove is harmless; an eagle flies high, and builds in the cliffs; a whippoorwill flies low, and sings his own song after sunset. And yet in not one of these instances did the individual, when young, give any indication as to what character it would take on further than a few very general things. If we see it with legs, we should judge it would walk, and that wings were intended for flying, etc.; but beyond this we learn nothing. And yet in all the countless myriads of instances we see the ox, the hog, the mule, the squirrel, the beaver, robin, swallow, etc., invariably despising all other habitudes and clinging, as with the grasp of death, to those of its own peculiar, exclusive race.

Now, what causes this wonderful and exact sameness in the character of all these several races? We do not know. For lack of knowledge, we give it the general name of Nature. It is *something*, we do not know what, that lies away back of itself.

Just so of man. There he is, just born; he has done nothing, said nothing, knows nothing; he has indicated neither a malevolent nor a benevolent disposition. It is true that pretty soon he shows that he has wants, and is impatient, and capable of anger; but he shows also that he is capable of government; and if left to the bent of his nature, he is about as likely to become a sinner as a dog is to become a barker, or a mocking-bird a singer.

And the same law rules in the vegetable kingdom. There is a plant a quarter of an inch high. It, of itself, has given not the slightest indication as to what it will grow to be. We have not the least idea whether it will grow a hundred feet high, live a hundred years, and bear nuts, or crawl a brief life on the ground of a few months, and bear pumpkins. It is only by ascertaining the race to which it belongs, and by comparing it with others of the same race, that we ascertain that this will bear apples, that potatoes, and the other corn.

Just so of man. We know he will be—not that he is, but that he will be—a sinner, be-

Conversion, or New Birth. 181

cause we see that he belongs to a race among whom sin is as universal, when not prevented by outside agency, as cabbage-heads among cabbage-stalks, or as crowing and cackling in a hen-roost.

This outside agency is provided, and needs only to be applied. It is the grace of God in salvation by Christ. Without it, sin and ruin are certain; with it, both may be averted.

Now, what precise words might or might not be used to describe this universal sinful tendency brings up questions more of biblical or theological criticism than of practical, moral, and religious utility.

Man is born not to sin, or with a necessity of sinning, nor for the purpose of sinning, but with a tendency, or inclination, to sin. This tendency is fixed and certain, but that does by no means prove that he *must* sin; nor is it proof positive that he *will* sin. He has a certain tendency that way, which, if not checked and prevented in time from ripening, will certainly ripen into a sinful life; and in this age of the world, and in the course of our observation, we have so uniformly seen it ripen that way that we hastily conclude it must be so. There is no absolute must, or necessity, in the case. Let this tendency be checked, and thoroughly arrested, the earlier the better, and let a religious—that is, an obedient—tendency be set up in its stead, and then the prospect is different. And what I insist is, that there is no *necessity* for waiting any number of years, neither one nor forty, for a more fit time for conversion. To wait a year is a disadvantage; to wait two years is still worse; and three, or ten, or forty, is still worse. Bring them up, not from a late period, but from the first, in the nurture and admonition of the Lord.

Admonition is instruction in duties, caution, direction. Let it begin at the first. In other words, let conversion take place at the proper time. Do not contentedly suffer the child to live at all in sin. Let him be converted as early as practicable—that is, the first year, month, or day, whether you can designate it or not. I have tried my best, and can frame no better rule to go by than this: Bring him up in the nurture and admonition of the Lord. This rule is neglected—nay, violated—in all cases of bad, angry, disobedient, or unconverted children, *of any age*.

CHAPTER XXVI.

CHILD'S FAITH AND CONVERSION.

THAT my observations on this head may be as intelligible as is desired, it is expedient to begin with some general remarks on the subject.

No religious theory, either for children or grown people, need be looked for in this essay that does not begin with the new birth, regeneration, or, if any prefer it, conversion. And yet this conversion is oftentimes viewed erroneously and disadvantageously by many persons. While it is always the proper beginning of religion, it is often the beginning of a very poor religion, and which soon turns out to be none at all. Many persons console themselves with the reflection that they *have been* converted. This consideration alone furnishes no ground whatever for consolation. The mere historic fact is of no value. It may be that one person who *was* and one who was not converted, and other things now equal, stand upon the same ground precisely. For conversion to be of any value, it must be *continuous*.

Is the person *now* converted? That is the only consideration of value. To take a proper step in the right direction of a long journey, and the continuing to walk in it, are very different things. The advantage is with him only who holds out to the end.

And again, we are sometimes taught that it is of very great, if not indispensable, advantage that we remember and can specify the day, hour, time, and place of the conversion. But then we must not forget that we can take cognizance only of our own doings and experience, and not the doings of the Almighty. The latter are not phenomenal at all. It is only the effect of conversion, or regeneration, that we feel. And then again, as we hope presently to see, if people were converted at the right time, or somewhere near the right time, it would be impracticable ever to remember the time and place of the conversion. The person would not remember a time when he was not converted. Conversion is the beginning, not the completion, of a religious life.

Again, we hear of "powerful conversions." And these are by some considered by far the best or most satisfactory kind. The meaning is, that the converted person is greatly or powerfully agitated, or exercised, in mind. However satisfactory it may be for a person to identify his conversion by strongly-exhibited marks, I cannot regard such conversions as the most satisfactory, or generally the most enduring. Certainly the best and most satisfactory conversions that can be are those which take place at or near the most proper time—that is, the earliest time—and consequently those that make the least exhibition on the outward person. A child converted at two years old has certainly, all though life, a great advantage, other things equal, of one converted at ten, or twenty, or a later period; provided always that the converted state be well maintained.

The longer a person continues to roam in sinful indulgences, be it a year or forty years, the poorer Christian he makes. This is inevitable. The very knowledge of his past sins, as well as the almost omnipotent power of habit, which he never can get entirely free from, continues to follow and haunt him as closely as his personal identity. Who has not observed that persons converted late in life very seldom possess the fullness and vigor of active Christianity that would have followed a life of early piety? The constitution of human nature has something to do with men.

While conversion, or new birth, is of itself always the same, the outward, or sensible, effects of it are as dissimilar as human temperament, circumstances, and disposition, are dissimilar. No two are alike. Look, then, at the conversion of a child of two years and a man of forty. The former has less disturbing, conscientious remembrance of sins committed than the latter. The comparison is as the Mississippi River compared to one of its rills. His conversion was specific, clear, genuine, but it was seen, felt, or experienced, as a gentle breath compared with a tornado; or, they may be compared thus: There are two oaks—both are crooked, and require to be straightened, and nothing more. The one is a quarter of an inch high, soft, and tender as wax; still it is crooked, and requires only to be straightened—the force of the most poetic zephyr, or the weight of a dew-drop, is sufficient; and now it is straight, and in becoming so has made no great noise nor created any great alarm in the world. And the other, in like manner, is only crooked, and requires only the same kind of process; but look at it: it is a hundred feet high, the giant peer of the clouds; its branches have defied the storms of a hundred winters; its limbs gnarled and knotted—some of them are two or three feet in diameter, and see how very crooked they have grown! Now, straighten that tree, and you require the force of a hurricane, or an engine of a thousand horse-power, or both, and the operation will wake up the neighborhood round about. There is a difference in these straightenings.

Now, who will not say, What a pity that tree was not straightened when it was tender and only a quarter of an inch high? That's when trees ought to be straightened, and when people ought to be converted. And then let the straightened tendril, whether tree or child, be kept straight—brought up in the way he should go. One conversion under three or four years is worth six at twelve, twenty at twenty, or forty at forty.

When we notice the efforts often made for the conversion of persons, either congregations or individuals, day after day, and year after year, and then see that those same persons, ministers or not, probably never spent an hour, or the tenth part of it, in direct labor for the conversion of children under eight or ten years, is not the impression irresistible that they do not consider small children subjects of converting grace at all? I have heard ministers of my Church relate remarkable instances of "early piety," when boys or girls of nine or ten years gave good evidence of regeneration, thus proving that early piety ought to be taught and promoted. And I have been mortified to see men who knew so little think they knew something. They would hardly listen to the idea of a child being converted at the age of four or five. Why, they would say—at least their conduct would say—"He hasn't been sinning more than two or three years; how could he be converted? Moreover, his conversion was not *powerful* enough; neither does he relate it in the regular, accepted, revival forms of language."

The doctrine evinced by the practice of many of us is that a child cannot be considered converted until he can stand a pretty good theological examination on the subject of the new birth, and use a good deal of Mr. Watson's language in regard to it; and so, not being able to do this at the age of eight or ten, he must of course be presumed to be unconverted, and treated as such, whether or no. Whereas, it seems plain to me that a child ought to be converted long before he is old enough to know theologically, or otherwise specifically, or in-

CHILD'S FAITH AND CONVERSION. 189

tellectually, any thing about conversion. Cannot a child feel an impulse before he knows that there is such a word as impulse? Cannot a child be sorry before he can describe sorrow by language? Children learn language at a very late period. They know every thing else before they begin to learn words.

In the very last letter I have from my wife she relates in regard to a grandchild, not yet two years old, how much he knew, with not the ability to speak a word. All moderately smart children are almost perfectly well acquainted with every thing they have seen or heard long before they can talk. How little we know about our children! Notice the well-taught child at family-prayer, or the blessing at table. He understands devotion as well as he ever will. I knew a boy of three years who on one occasion had inadvertently turned up his plate at table before saying his *Mylordy*, and he peremptorily refused to receive his food. His plate must be returned empty and placed in the usual position, and when he said his *Mylordy*, then let it be turned up and helped. This was done with all apparent devotional concern. Is there any better religion than that? The Saviour recommended it for adoption by the apostles.

Was ever a person converted at the right time within your knowledge? Of course the conversion, no matter when, is well; but how much better would it have been a year before, or a year before that, or before that, or before that! The right time is the best time.

CHAPTER XXVII.

CHILDREN ONCE CONVERTED.

REGENERATION is a better term than conversion, especially when applied to a small child. Of course this is the starting-point for all Christianity. But alas! we know but too well that the cases of Christian life and death are by no means to be numbered with the instances of regeneration. My own belief is that the former are few, while the latter are many. If we could see the comparison we should be startled with amazement. My belief is that among us generally nowadays not one regeneration in ten or twenty, or perhaps in forty or more, results well. And especially is this the case among children. The children of pious parents who receive reasonable religious instruction are pretty generally regenerated early in life.

In the first place, not one-tenth part the instrumental labor and force is required to bring small children into the Christian faith as those of ten or fifteen years or more; and in the second, far more constant oversight is required to maintain it. Children, no matter how religious, are thoughtless, volatile, and fickle.

There is a pious mother, with children grown and growing up around her, whose life is weighed down with sorrow because they are all irreligious. They were every one converted by her own pious labors in the lullaby lessons and prayers she taught them when the soft, wax-like heart received the simple truths greedily; but alas! the poor woman, following the drift and fashion around her, said to herself —if she thought at all, which is by no means certain: "Dear little ones, too young, far too young, to be religious now; but I hope they will become religious when they get old enough." And so, considering, or seeming to consider, that outside the Church, among bad boys and girls, is the best place for children to maintain a religious life, with the consent and approval of father and pastor, the children are thrust out of the Church. The religion she has so well assisted to establish is neither recognized nor encouraged, and shipwreck is about as likely to take place as in an attempt to navigate Niagara Falls.

The child was not conscious of his religion in any scientific or theological sense. He knew what he felt, though he could not by any means describe it, and, with no one to explain and encourage him, it never occurred to him that that was what the grown people call religion. It never occurred to him, because he had never been taught it, that a little boy could have religion—that is, such religion as they talk and preach about in the Church. He supposed that all there was for him to do was to be good—tolerably good—and wait till he should grow old enough to be religious. And when he grew into his teens, these tender feelings—to which he did not attach much importance at the first, because not so taught—are all dissipated, and the religion to which he looked forward with some solicitude is all gone, gone, gone over the hills and far away. He is a confirmed backslider, a veteran in sin, and, nine cases in ten, a settled hater of Christ.

I have known several melancholy illustrations of these things. Some years ago, the eldest child of two persons, whom I would class among the most pious and discreet people I have known, was a girl—an unusually smart child. At the age of three, four, and five, and along there, she gave the most clear and satisfactory evidence of divine grace and faith. Some instances I heard related of her faith and power in prayer were remarkable and convincing. She is now a grown woman, educated and accomplished, and—an infidel.

And does any one say this is strange? How is this? I think it is most natural, and nothing is more easily accounted for. She grew up outside the Church. And the man who looks 'for much religious fruit outside the Church has something yet to learn of human nature. The returns to the Church and to piety, under such circumstances, are the exceptions—rather rare exceptions; the shipwrecks and loss are the rule.

Not long since, I asked a Methodist preacher to buy some religious books, reminding him that his boys—three grown young men—might need them. "O," said he, "my boys are all infidels; they would not read a religious book!" I was not at all startled at such an announcement, for I saw the cause plainly. The father and mother were exemplary, pious; the children were converted in the nursery at the mother's knee, and then turned out to imbibe the out-of-the-Church religion, and to expect Church-religion—when they should grow old enough!

I know a young man, piously reared, of much more than ordinary intellectual capacity, a veteran infidel. He was one of the very best and most pious children I ever knew; but he took the usual course.

Now, if any one thinks these uncommon cases—exceptions to the general rule—he is greatly mistaken. With more or less variation, this is the condition of four-fifths of all the young people around us, and older ones too, who were brought up by pious parents. They may not be strictly infidel, but they are solidly irreligious.

The cure for all this is plain, and the means are at hand. *Bring the children up in* the nurture and admonition of the Lord. Instead of this we bring them up out of it, with the hope of getting them into it after they grow up. Nineteen times in twenty, this is a vain hope.

CHAPTER XXVIII.

CONVERSION—JOINING CHURCH.

I HAVE argued that it is the absolute duty of all men to be in the Church. This follows necessarily and logically upon the supposition that Christianity is an undeviating rule of conduct. The two propositions are but different modes of stating the same thing. Then, you might as well inquire if this or that person is eligible to tell the truth, to be virtuous, to keep the commandments, as to inquire if he is eligible to Church-membership. To inquire whether this or that person ought now to be in the Church, or is eligible to membership by reason of age, stature, moral fitness, or any other reason, is to show that the inquirer has yet to learn what the Church *is*.

1 have a reverend and venerable friend and brother who, if I understand him rightly, is a little troubled on this subject. Conversion, he thinks, must go first, and Church-membership afterward, following a personal application for it, and be accompanied by an approved statement of experience. And there may be others

hampered in the same way. My friend, once upon a time, illustrated his objections to membership before a profession of faith in an argument embodying the following poser:

On a rail-car he chanced to sit beside a nice little girl of perhaps twelve years, and introduced a conversation, intending to give it a religious turn. He inquired of her home, parents, etc. Her father was a Baptist, her mother a Christian, as was also an elder sister. And then ensued the following questions and answers:

"And do you belong to the Church?"

"O yes, sir."

"When were you converted?"

"I do not know, sir."

"Did you repent of your sins, and pray to God for Christ's sake to forgive your sins?"

"No, sir."

"Then, why did you join the Church?"

"Well, I always learned that I ought to believe in Jesus Christ as the Saviour, and be baptized, and then I would be in the Church; and I thought this was right, and did so."

"Now," said my friend, "look at that picture. That is the character of a Church of unconverted persons. You say 'everybody ought to be in the Church.' This girl, mistaken and deluded, is in the Church. What sort of Church will you soon have?"

My reply is this: First, from what my friend stated of this little girl, I do not know whether she was or was not converted, or had been converted. I incline to regard her a good Christian girl, but do not know. Quite likely she had been converted, and may or may not have been at that time. She was certainly a good girl, religiously inclined, whose religious instruction had probably been but poor, and likely much neglected. Few men of large religious experience have not known persons of far more age and experience than this child, of sound internal holy life, and who would not have sufficient self-confidence to declare promptly to his or her pastor, and much less to a stranger, in categorical answer to a direct question, "I am converted." Young Christians are generally timid and hesitating.

I am sorry if my friend has yet to learn that there are many pious children whose piety you must learn, if at all, in a more indirect and delicate manner than by a bold and open question, put by an elderly man, an entire stranger, in a momentary rail-car conversation. Few religious children would have answered more promptly than she did. My friend is a Boanerges, confident and outspoken, of three-score and ten years, and more, and the replicant a timid child, a little girl of twelve years, in the presence of a stranger.

Secondly: The child had probably never had the advantage of better religious training than an unfavorable view of her answers would indicate. But it is marvelous my friend should have so entirely failed to discover *what* the religious error of this child was. In this unfavorable view of the case, the little girl was certainly in error, and, though it was as big as a barn-door, my reverend friend strangely failed to see it. Overlooking her real fault, he blamed her for *doing right*—for obeying God. That she ought to have joined the Church when she did, I do not see how any Christian can question. As to this matter, her blame was—or that of her parents—that she did not join long before.

She certainly did right in joining the Church, and as certainly did wrong in failing to do another thing of vital importance. As is the case with thousands—whether in the Church or not is not important—she probably failed to *be religious*, or, in Scripture language, to become converted. She did one thing right, exactly right—a more proper thing never was done by mortal man—but failed to do another vitally important thing. Her error was not as to what she *did*, but what she failed to do. And these two things being coïnherent and coëssential, the thing done availed nothing, in all likelihood.

If my friend had continued the conversation with the little girl, which he no doubt would if there had been opportunity, it would of course have been on this wise:

"My dear Miss, I am sorry to see you in such religious error as you represent. I am an old man, as you see, and a minister. I have had much experience among religious people, and if you will listen to my advice it may be of lasting benefit to you. I am glad to see you religiously inclined, for it is a good thing for young people, as well as older ones, to be religious; but you did very wrong in joining the Church—that was very irreligious. None but converted people must join the Church. It is very well to join the Church after conversion, but very sinful to do it before. People must be converted outside the Church, not in it. Inside the Church is the place to live a religious life, but not the place to become religious. The place, and the only true and proper place, to become religious, or more pious, is outside, among irreligious people. Inside the Church is a very bad place to be converted. The rule is, to become converted first, and join the Church afterward. Now, my young friend, remember this, and act accordingly.

"So, the proper course for you to pursue is, first to undo the wrong you have done—go out of the Church. Go immediately to your pastor, and tell him to take your name off the list of members; and if he asks you why, tell him frankly you want to get converted. Tell him you have learned much more about this matter than you knew before—that you have had the subject explained by a Methodist minister. And you may intimate too, very decidedly, if you wish—for that is true—that the Methodist divines know much more concerning these subjects than the Baptists or the Christians do. Go out of the Church first, and out there among irreligious people, among sinners like yourself, pray, and repent of your sins, and when you seek religion long enough, God will convert your soul. And when it is certain you are converted, and the pastor is perfectly satisfied, he will then take you in. Then you will be right."

This is the doctrine of my friend. He wants to keep the Church pure. He does not believe —to use his own words—"the Church is a hospital," a place for people to grow better, or improve and rise from a low and defective religious state to a higher and more healthy state of grace. This would degrade the Church, in his estimation.

And there stands my friend to-day, a doctor of divinity, and minister of high standing, and that is the teaching with which he teaches teachers, and instructs others, and leads the young and tender lambs. How can Christianity be looked for among our children amidst such preaching as this?

I believe the doctrine *"Be sure you are converted before you join the Church"* is most dangerous and destructive to Christianity. And why our religious authors, newspapers, bishops, and ministers, do not drive it from the Church is, I think, because they do not look at it fully in the face.

This is not a question, as many seem to suppose, of mere Church purity or impurity. It is a question respecting the field or domain of the pastor's labor. Is this confined to the Church? Is it his exclusive duty to look after the purity of the Church? or, does a part of it lie outside in labors to disciple outsiders? The latter, most assuredly. And even if this be left out of the account, is the purity and religiousness of the Church best promoted by "guarding the doors" so as to keep out persons of honest religious proclivity and intuition, whose experience has risen no higher than a sincere desire to flee from the wrath to come, and be saved? There are many such persons, and a vitally important question is, Will their religious state be most likely to improve outside or in? I insist that outside is an unfavorable place *to do any thing*. The faithful and intelligent pastor always encourages the entrance into the Church of all persons who could or would join in good faith. Good faith could not mean less than a sincere desire to be saved. Church coldness, worldliness, or irreligion of any sort, is best cured *in the Church*. Or, if not, *turn them out!* Be consistent.

CHAPTER XXIX.

OF CHILD'S FAITH.

RELIGIOUS, or what is often called saving, faith does not necessarily include even a correct A B C of theological knowledge. A child's faith must of course come down to a child's condition. He does not know A B C literally, nor figuratively, applied to any thing. He has neither physical nor literary ability to pronounce a word of his mother-tongue intelligibly; and how could he be expected to know more about the external things of Christianity than other matters of knowledge?

He knows nothing about a revelation, nor about many other things pertaining to the very rudiments of religion, and yet, though at first it may to some seem contradictory, he is quite far advanced in real substantial religious knowledge.

Whatever may be said about the natural tendency to sin, call it by what name you will, and his certainty to drift into it—yea, and wallow in it—in the absence of proper early religious training, he has a far earlier and greater precocity for the acquisition of religious knowledge than of any other kind. You can teach a child religion—most valuable things about religion—long before you can teach him any thing else outside the narrowest cradle or nursery limits. There is something planted in children by Nature, I suppose, favorable to the acquisition of the most valuable religious knowledge; yea, and religious sentiments and feelings too. This is not faith, nor piety, but an aptitude or fitness for the very early reception of religious knowledge, reverence, and holy feelings.

Children, in ordinarily favorable circumstances, well cared for, will have a keen sense of religious reverence, awe, and some sense of religious responsibility, by about the close of the first or second year. A neglected, fretting, frisking child, or one who has been handled and dawdled only as a doll, and knows nothing except to *be pleased* with toys, will witness the evening prayer of an older sister, or a mother, and will keep frisking about, whining, and looking to be pleased, caring nothing for what is going on. You will often see a child of three or four years, in a religious family, that cannot be kept still at family-prayer. The poor neglected child has never been taught any thing but to be pleased with toys and prattle.

Young children are wonderfully imitative, and if well cared for will soon catch the idea of prayer, and at once almost can be impressed with the reverence and awe of devotion. There is a wonderful aptness for it, if not an instinct in it. A well-taught child of two or three years has a perception and recognition of devotion as clear as he is likely to acquire afterward. And let him be properly trained and cared for, and mothers of not more than ordinary carelessness will be surprised to find how early the little fellow will take in the idea of devotion; and it will be with the child not a mere something to look at, but it will be *devotion*, distinct and separate from all other considerations.

To the great mass of parents who know almost nothing about such things, it would be truly wonderful to know how little well-directed attention is required to inculcate in very small children sentiments and feelings of true religion. They understand what is going on at church as well as anybody does. Preparations for family-prayer awe them into silence, and inspire them with reverence. Many who have never studied the character of children regard this as a mere habit of keeping still. It may be so with neglected or carelessly managed children, but with a child properly managed it is true devotion. He thinks about God, and about being good; he reflects that God is very good, and is now looking upon him. His clear and distinct thoughts about being good, and the necessity of it, are in the clearest and most wakeful activity. If spoken to about God's *will*, he might not understand you, but he knows very well what God *wants*, and he is earnestly endeavoring to do what God wants him to do; and when his devotional thoughts are awake, he would not do otherwise. In long services, he becomes wearied with stillness, and may go to sleep. Children act by moments, not by hours.

That simple, unhesitating obedience in recognition of God and in subserviency to him is what I understand to constitute the faith recommended in the gospel. Away with that unscriptural and enthusiastic notion which postpones early Christianity until a later and more intellectual period—that teaches that "children will be wicked anyhow, being created in sin!" I know of nothing that we have to do about the creation of children. They are already created before we have any thing to do with them. Our business is to bring them up in, not out of, the nurture and admonition of the Lord.

I know of nothing either in the nature or usual practical character of Christian faith that is not of a high order in a well-taught child of tender years, even long before he could give a plausible definition of it.

A child was once brought into court to testify as a witness in an important case. The lawyers said: "O the boy is too young, too young entirely. It is preposterous — a mocking of justice." The judge took up the little fellow into his lap, and talked with him about some familiar matter, and let him see some other witnesses sworn. He then asked the little boy, in presence of the lawyers, if he knew what it was to take an oath. The lisping child answered, *"Da mus' tell de truf."* The judge decided promptly that there was no incompetency because of age. The chief-justice of the nation could not give a better answer. But if they had gone on further to catechise the child, and ask him what truth was, he might have been as much puzzled for an answer as Pilate was. And so, if we were to catechise a child as to what faith is, he might give as poor an answer as some of Paul's interpreters make him give. There are some things — many things—that children know as well as grown men and women ever can know. A child with three apples gives one to a sister—he knows he has two, and no more, left. He knows that as well as the astutest mathematician knows it, yet he could not tell what subtraction means.

Just so of religious obligation. No one can understand what religious obligation is better than a child, though he could not describe it. I repeat that it is worthy of all grave consideration that the very first thing a child can understand outside the simple nursery routine is religious obligation — obligation to God — that God requires him to *do right*. And that God requires us to do right is the highest and weightiest religious obligation I know any thing about. The child who would desist from doing something he wanted to do because God would be displeased if he should do it is a Christian of a high stamp.

But the faith of a child is of a very high order of purity, from the very consideration that he is a child of great inexperience. A man has had his mind poisoned with a thousand considerations — if they could be accurately counted they would amount to millions—interposing doubts about religious obligation in a thousand forms. He has all these to overcome, but the child has not. The child receives religious instruction with the utmost reverence, and with no more doubt about the truth of it than of his own being. He has not the least hesitation. Perplexing doubts never disturbed him; infidelity never disturbed him; German and French free-thinkers, and the trumpet-tongued Humes and Paines, have never assailed him. He has not read the plausible nonsense and gilt-edged lying monstrosities of Huxley, Tyndal, and Ecce Homo; nor has the infidelity of novel-reading attacked him. Neither have his passions—strong, stalwart, and ferocious—surrounded him, and threatened his capture and his overthrow. His heart is soft, susceptible, and not preöccupied. Where can be found the man or woman, or even the boy or girl of twelve years, in so favorable a condition to imbibe and enjoy the simple faith of Christ?

A child should never be permitted to go out from the confines of the nursery among all sorts of people, mixing with bad books, bad words, bad conduct, and bad thoughts, without having his mind and heart well stored with true evangelical faith in God. And this faith must not be mistaken; it must not be a loose, undefined system of negative keeping-still conduct, generally acceptable to the rest of the family, but religious faith. A child of three years—perhaps not your child, but a well-instructed child of three years or under—can as well understand his obligations to God as he can twenty years later.

Taking the great and diversified natural constitution as I find it, with such examination as I have been able to make of it in a life of some length and some activity, I am unable to see any better, if indeed any other, use for the period of nursery-life than to use its seclusion for the very grand purpose of getting a good start of the devil in religious bracings, and laying the strong and solid foundations of high evangelical faith. I know not of the impediment in making bones and muscles grow as much in two years as they usually do in twenty, but I do not see how the safeguards of the nursery could be dispensed with in the best formations of the best religious faith.

Surely the best existing faith to be found now anywhere is that which received its strong granite foundation and massive bracings in the nursery. Other things equal, no man can fail to see that the man of faith all through life, who *had* a strong nursery faith to carry, and did and does carry it, unsullied, unshattered, is the better Christian therefor. Paul would have been a better Christian if he had had it, and so would David, and so would any man.

Faith formed at a late period has necessarily to contend against many and immense disadvantages of preöccupation. No wonder the Saviour recommended nursery faith; because it is, and cannot fail to be, the best.

Christian culture and agriculture have great similarity in many important respects. In both cases the weeds spring up and begin to grow simultaneously with the true plant; in both cases the earlier the destruction of the former begins the better; and in both cases constant cultivation is alike necessary. Let the agricultor suffer the weeds and grass to grow, and constantly take deeper and deeper root, attaining greater and greater strength, until the true plant has attained one-fourth or one-third of its growth, and now two things are easily seen: first, for even the most moderate growth double, treble, or quadruple the labor is necessary; and, secondly, a full growth of the plant is impossible. The time is past. The analogy between the two cultures is perfect.

But it may be objected that children believe in Christianity merely because they are told so—they would as readily believe the wildest romance. This is very true. The difference is that the Christianity they believe *is true*, the romance is not. What matters it how credulous a person may be so that he believes what is true? Religion is just as true without as with a logical and intelligible assent. A child can tell you that the sun is ninety-five million miles distant; and if so taught, he would tell you it was ninety-five miles distant. The difference is that the one is true and the other is not. The great object is, that we know the truth; the means or method by which we come to know it is quite unimportant. Truth is as important acquired one way as another.

CHAPTER XXX.

THE RIGHT TIME FOR CONVERSION.

ANY thing that ought to be done at all ought to be done at the right time. Conversion—the commencement of a religious life—ought to take place at the right time. The disadvantage of passing by the right time to begin a religious life *can never be overcome.* Men and women of late conversion may pass along very well, as it may be considered, and may succeed in getting to heaven; but whether one may know it or not, he is never the man he would have been if more years of religious experience had been added at the beginning. This is the cause of most of the irresolution, the feebleness, lack of value to the Church, lack of devotion, lack of family religion, which we see and mourn over, in the Church all around us.

No man attains the full proficiency for which nature endowed him, either in moral or physical enterprise, who does not embark in it in childhood. The earlier the better. Our ideas —many of us—of the giant strength of habit,

The Right Time for Conversion. 215

especially of sinful habit, are entirely too feeble and diluted. Sin is not a matter of so small import as many of us suppose. The child of five or eight years is a giant and a veteran in iniquity. Not so when he was one, two, or three. The very best years of the whole life-time are lost never to be regained.

Instead of considering these things properly, many of us seem by our conduct to regard early sinfulness up to twelve, or fifteen, or twenty, as a sort of necessary matter-of-course; but little religious, well-directed labor is bestowed upon children of such ages, and we consider ourselves remarkably fortunate if our children be brought back to the Church and to God by the time they are twenty.

Men of observation are well aware that occasionally children of three or four years have given satisfactory evidence of converting grace —either grace to live with or grace to die with, perhaps more particularly the latter. It is with children as with men or women—grace uniformly develops to outward observation far more fully on the near approach of death than at any other time. And we know very well, or at least will see very clearly if we look into the subject a little, that converting grace is very likely to exist in children long before we can discover any satisfactory outward evidences of it.

This results from two causes: first, the child himself is not able, from mere intellectual incapability, to discover, identify, and recognize a state of conversion as a distinct, separate, and specific state. He recognizes something and feels religious, but does not know but everybody feels that way. He has never heard and studied elaborate descriptions of the unconverted and the converted states as those of us have who have for hundreds of times seen them held up in contrast with each other. A clear knowledge of sinful life as a state, apart from incidental acts of wrongdoing, and the opposite, are things to be learned as matter of information; they do not come by mere intuition. These considerations cannot be enforced too strongly, or repeated too often. Secondly, our means of communicating with small children about such matters are very slim. They can but very feebly describe their feelings of aches and pains in sickness. They cannot describe any thing very well. If thirsty, they cannot tell you so; they can only utter general complaint, or hunt for and point out the dipper or pitcher. If tired and sleepy, the

The Right Time for Conversion. 217

child cannot tell you. He feels bad, but hardly knows why.

To be able to feel and to describe one's feelings are very different things. The one does by no means necessarily imply the other. Small children have very little knowledge of life and the world around them. Ninety-nine hundredths of all the preaching is to get the people to unlearn the vicious things they have learned in the several years of a vicious life. Young children have very little of this to unlearn.

Was any person ever converted *at the right time* that we know of? Better late than never, it is true; but would it not have been better at an earlier period? Look at our revivals—our numbers converted and added to the Church as reported from our meetings; and where are they in a year? in a month? in a day? or, I may well add, within an hour afterward? Their conversions were right enough, with one very important exception. It was at a wofully bad time. That mountain of unhallowed experience fastening on the converted boy or girl, habits of error piled up like mountains, are a heavy burden to carry. If these conversions had occurred at a better time, things would be very different. It is hard to reap figs where thistles were sown and cultivated.

I would greatly like to see a Church of a hundred members all young converts, where not one knew when he was converted—he had been religious from his earliest recollection; he does not know when he was not religious. What an array of Christian soldiers this would be! The public effect of such a Church would be overwhelming.

And will any one say this is croaking, asking too much, or speculating about religion? So far from it, every one will acknowledge that these things ought to be; and therefore it is the duty of all Christian men and women to aim at that point and labor for it. On the contrary, we are most of us asleep on the great subject of early piety, so vitally important to the Church. Indeed, many of us hardly seem to know there is, or can be, such a thing. Many of us call youthful piety early piety. Many of us have been so superficially taught as almost to be unwilling to recognize piety in small children at all.

The loss to the Church, to family piety, to the cause of Christ, from this one consideration, is believed to be fearfully great. The most that is generally aimed at with children under twelve years of age is to get them to behave well—that is, to commit no outrage of a

The Right Time for Conversion. 219

flagrant character; and people, even pious people, are generally very content with this absence of high crime. They are counted good children. Parents congratulate themselves. Of course this is better than the criminality we so often see around us in our families, but it falls so far short of Christian duty and Christian privilege that, looked at carefully, it is lamentable. It establishes in parents and children, and general society, as well as in the Church, a habit, custom, and moral tone that are in the highest degree damaging.

A child of fourteen has had ten long years, by far the longest and best of the entire life, of well-recognized or tolerated out-of-the-Church irreligion. He has lived this long with the well-settled idea, strengthening and strenghtening every day, that that was a very proper way to live. This irreligious out-of-the-Church habitude has acquired far more strength in this period than it could in any other decade of his life—yea, more than in all combined.

One-twentieth part of the labor necessary to bring a man of twenty-five into the Church, if well, properly, and continuously directed, would have kept him in from the first. Prevention is more efficacious than cure. Ninety-nine hundredths of the wickedness in children is the result of parental and pastoral neglect. Of course weeds will grow; but the agriculturist was put there with muscle and means to destroy them.

The Saviour said to Peter, "Feed my sheep;" and he also said, "Feed my lambs." Each expression has its meaning. One thing in common with the feeding of *sheep* and *lambs* is that they are both to be fed inside the fold—not the sheep inside, and the lambs out. This is unnatural, and was never intended. The lambs are to be fed as well as the sheep; and in doing so, proper care is to be observed that both the food and the feeding be adapted and arranged to suit the lamb-like capacity of the tenderer ones. The proper feeding of sheep would be of little or no advantage to the lambs. Nor is it enough, as we generally do, to suffer the lambs to be present, a few of them, and let them witness the ceremony of feeding the sheep. They must themselves be fed.

Many preachers—might I not say most of us—as a quaint writer expresses it, seem greatly to misapprehend the Saviour's meaning when he said, "Feed my lambs." They understand him to mean, *Feed my giraffes.* Now, a giraffe, otherwise called a camelopard, is a very tall animal, with an enormous length of neck. His food is most convenient for him when placed about eighteen or twenty feet high, and the rough boughs and bark suit him well for food. That kind of food would not suit lambs. Their food must be of a tenderer sort, and be placed down on or near the ground. The Saviour did not allude to giraffes. He meant *lambs*, and directed that they should be fed.

CHAPTER XXXI.

OF CHURCH-MEMBERSHIP.

IF the Church were an institution set up by authority—either divine or human authority—in the nature of a corporation with a charter; that is, some fundamental laws of government, such institution being instrumentally designed to promote Christianity, as High-churchmen teach—if this were the character of the Church, then there would be room for questions of eligibility to membership in it. Such an institution must of course have conditions of membership. They might be the payment of dues; requisite age, sex, or color; so much religion, to be judged of by a committee; the performance of certain duties, or the like. Then a compliance with these conditions, whatever they might be, would open the door of admission. All that is easily understood. Then we have only to turn to the constitution, and see if the applicant comes up to the conditions. He may or may not be eligible.

But when I see the Church is not an institution of this kind at all; that it has not and never had a charter, or law of government; that it is merely a Christian brotherhood, the segregation and congregation of Christian people brought together by the spontaneous gravitation and coherence of Christian love and religious. principle—when I see that this is the character of the Church, then I see no place for questions about personal eligibility. We might as well talk about persons being eligible to truth-telling as to Church-membership. It is simply a duty.

When I see the Church never had, and in its nature never could have, prescribed conditions precedent of membership, and no conditions of membership or social coherence at all other than such as naturally and necessarily inhere in the very idea of personal Christianity, and make up its very essence—when I see these plain things, how can I see room for questions whether this or that person is legally eligible to Church-membership?

The relation of baptized children to the Church, who are irreligious, is the same as any other irreligious baptized persons, who repudiate and ignore their solemn religious vows. Where the blame rests, is another question. The fault is not with the baptism or the membership, but the personal conduct. It is like any other case of backsliding. Human persons ought to be in the Church, because that is a universal duty; but that does not imply that irreligious conduct ought to be in the Church.

It is the gravitation and segregation of Christianity that forms the Church; but this cannot prevent the occasional, or even frequent, introduction of unworthy material. Indeed, all the material in the Church is, in a very important sense, unworthy, and it is the duty of the Church to reform itself, the lowest as well as the highest. The Church is not the result of legislation, nor of adjudication, but is the spontaneous moving of individual hearts toward God and each other under the movings of the Holy Ghost. The Church is natural, not legal, and forms itself by its own spontaneity.

And if religion appertains to children, why does not the Church? It would be mere violence to separate between the Church and Christianity. Religion and Church are not two separate and distinct things, each complete in itself; they are twin and coïnherent aspects of one and the same thing. The Church-membership of children, therefore, of whatever age, must be viewed in the light of that of other persons. Children are merely a part of mankind, and though not capable of commerce, mechanism, philosophy, or general industries, by reason of mental and physical nonage, they are fully capable of Christianity.

Children have rights too—rights of a high and sacred character. It is the sacred duty of parents to protect and defend their religious and ecclesiastical rights, as much so as any other rights. Their Church-rights are as valuable and dear to them as to the rest of us. The Saviour is in the Church, religion is in the Church, salvation is in the Church.

> When troubles rise, and storms appear,
> There may his children hide.

Bereave me of what else you may — valuable, near, dear as they may be, you may eliminate my name from among men, and take away the light of the sun from above me, and forbid me to walk upon the ground that is beneath me—but leave me, I pray you, the Church which my Saviour gave me. As it ought to be my first, let it be my last, boon of earth; and O in it deprive me not of my little ones!

And is the Church more valuable to me than to the little three-year-old prattler who has not had the opportunity of acquiring so much information respecting its value as I have? His lack of appreciation of his Church-rights is no more significant than the same lack respecting his rights of property, or any other franchises.

I was glad to see Bishop Marvin's remark:* "It is not a matter of small consequence what relation our children sustain to the Church—whether they shall come upon the arena of that contest in which eternal life is lost or won in their place in the militant host, or enter it single-handed and without support." Verily it is not!

While the folly of supposing the Church to possess and impart intrinsic grace is among the greatest of popular follies, and is certainly one of the most injurious Romish errors still lingering in some shapes among us, it is nevertheless true that the mere fact of membership in the Church exerts a most wonderfully beneficial effect upon the mind and heart of the young, as well as those who are older.

The notion of some is, or seems to be, that we should not bind our children in Church-membership, or matters of religion and con-

---

*When this was written, it was expected the Bishop would read it. But alas!

science. This is exceeding flimsy and thoughtless. So, then, we should not bind them to live in a certain neighborhood, lest when they grow up they might choose to live in some other, or in none. I must not bind my child to industry, for I do not know but he might prefer a lazy, indolent life; I must not bind him to habits of sobriety, for I do not know but he may prefer the life of a drunkard. And for the same reason I must not educate him; I must not bind him to decency and good manners, nor to obedience, nor truth-telling, and so forth. It might as well be said that we may not provide food, clothing, medicine, or any other necessary provision, as that we may neglect the children's Church-membership.

And yet how loosely is this high duty generally attended to! How few are in the Church! Most children of Methodist parents, we may presume, are baptized, but this "relation to the Church," as it is sometimes called, seems to be of no practical benefit. They grow up with it the same as without it. They are as clearly and fully out of the Church as those unbaptized. They grow up in open and well-recognized non-membership, and generally without a hope of conversion, except at some almost or quite adult period, by means of such general ministrations as are usually directed to veteran sinners.

The Sunday-school makes wholesome provision for this state of things as far as its instrumentality, as now organized, can reach it; but it reaches it slowly and imperfectly. Let us hope for such improvement as may render mere baptism something more than nominal. A proper home-discipline will find most children practically religious before they go to Sunday-school.

Our pastoral theology, what little we have amongst us relating to children, does not contemplate their conversion until a late period. It provides that first the child must be instructed in biblical history, geography, biography, etc., whereas it seems to me certain that the religion of the Bible should be first taught and well inculcated. This is where his earliest susceptibilities lie. The piety of Christianity can be solidly riveted in his little unsuspecting heart long before he can be taught much about Mesopotamia or the character of Esau. But by all means this should be done in the Church, not out it. It is of vast importance that children should understand that they are in the Church. They should be taught to fear the outside world; a knowledge of the mere fact that they are inside cannot fail to exert a powerful influence.

A child ought to be so trained—that is, it ought to be practicable for him to be so trained—as never to be subjected to the perplexing questions about joining the Church. Outside persons, young or old, somewhat religiously inclined, are constantly harassed with such questions as, When is he going to join; whether he feels like it; how long it may be safely deferred; whether the preacher is esteemed well enough; whether this or that person will join also; and many similar ones. Such questions benumb the sensibilities, and lessen the importance of Church-alliance.

Our system of child-culture would seem to be susceptible of improvement from the consideration that so few children of Methodist parents grow up, live, and die, in the Church. When Methodist children go to other Churches, it is for merely social or still more unworthy motives. But many go not even to other Churches; many grow up Church-haters.

For these evils it is easy to point out a remedy; the far greater difficulty is to provide the means of adopting it. Is not our ministerial labor directed proportionally too much to the Church, and not enough to the families?

But which preacher is to begin? Moreover, our Conference rules do not contemplate much, if any, labor among children—especially small children—where there is so much need for it. Practical innovation upon a routine is not so easy. The preachers generally do what they are expected, or what the rules require, but do not generally go beyond.

CHAPTER XXXII.

ON THE BAPTIZING OF CHILDREN.

ALL persons ought to be baptized. Proper subjects of baptism are human persons. Christ died for all. That settles the question of what ought to be the boundaries of the Church. All persons ought to acknowledge Christ.

But young children cannot apply for or accept baptism directly for themselves. It must be done for them, if at all, by parents, or other persons acting in the stead of parents. A minister could not pick up an unknown child in the street and baptize him. Baptism implies that there be recognition and record of it. It is an ecclesiastical act.

But we are told we must not baptize children of persons who are not believers. Who says so? and secondly, What is meant by "believers?" Infidel parents would not be likely to apply for, or desire, baptism for their children. Must the pastor judge of the precise necessary belief, or faith, of such parents—determine as to its doctrinal soundness and correctness of the profession of it? This would require a Romish priest, if not a pope. Must such parents be members of some Church? and what Church, as a condition precedent? As well as I can understand the matter, it amounts to about this: that we must not baptize a child unless the parents be religious enough. But precisely how religious, might be difficult to determine.

The fact that parents, or guardians, desire baptism for their children, or willingly accept it, would seem to settle the question of their belief so far as seems to be necessary for this purpose.

The baptism of young children or infants should not, it seems to me, be made a specialty, but regarded as mere baptism in general. I see no reference, either in Scripture or the reason of the thing, to infant baptism or adult baptism. I do not see two kinds, but only one. The Scriptures speak of *baptism*, and refer it to the human family with no particular reference to age, size, or sex. It makes no restriction. There is, however, this general principle to be observed: that a duty neglected to-day should be performed to-morrow. It is upon this principle that the baptism of grown people is recognized. Let baptism be attended to as it ought to be, and there could be no adult baptism. It is but a *dernier ressort* to remedy, as well as may be, a neglected duty back yonder. Baptism is for mankind; Christianity is for mankind.

CHAPTER XXXIII.

A REMEDY.

KEEP the children in the Church. If, through ignorance, negligence, or other incompetency of parents, or of pastors, we cannot keep all in, we can begin, or improve, and keep some in. Some of our best families and best pastors can set a most gracious and wholesome example. Do not wait until you can teach the little ones Bible-history, but begin early to teach the solid principles of Christianity. Teach religion first, and give them biblical information afterward as they may begin to be able to understand it. Early religious lessons should be few and short—the whole of religion can be comprehended in a very few words. The child has already graduated in the great and important science of obedience, and knows as much about that as he ever can know. He has already learned about God and Christ, and can very easily comprehend that God loves good children, that Christ died for them, and will take all good boys and girls up to heaven. Let the sister of five years be accustomed to teach her brother of three. No better assistant teacher is needed. Let these lessons be constant, and as well as may be at stated times, especially at bed-time. Let no day pass unimproved. It requires but a minute or two of time, and that not exclusive of other employment. Do not fail to let them understand all the while that they are in the Church. Do not turn them out, either formally or informally, actually or virtually. Teach the children all to notice carefully and distinguish between right actions and wrong ones. A complaining, scolding, threatening woman cannot do these things—neither can one who has not the time; but a prudent, intelligent woman, who regulates her household affairs well, and is sensibly and prayerfully alive to the importance of early piety, will find no difficulty whatever in giving full attention to all these things. She will be surprised to learn how easy it is when she tries it. The children will be ready and anxious for the evening or morning lessons. There will be nothing irksome or tiresome about it; every thing will be cheerful and pleasant.

One difficulty at present is that we have no catechism suited to the nursery; but somebody will make one. We have plenty for larger children, but none for beginners. Several persons have tried it, but I have not known one to succeed well, except one that never went into general use. This was written some years ago by the lamented Rev. R. S. Rosenbaugh, late of the Memphis Conference. It was the best I have seen, but it never went, so far as I know, beyond the columns of the *Western Methodist*, then published at Memphis, Tenn.

Bishop Marvin's words are worthy to be remembered and repeated: "God has ordained in the Church many efficient aids, many means of grace, through which the earnest penitent and more advanced believer are alike strengthened and helped forward in the Christian race. The fellowship of saints and the ordinances of religion quicken the spiritual perception and sensibilities, and encourage and strengthen faith. The mere fact of membership in the Church exerts a most wholesome effect on the mind and heart. It is not a matter of small consequence what relation our children shall sustain to the Church—whether they shall come upon the arena of that contest in which eternal life is lost or won in their place in the militant host, or enter it single-handed and without support." These are wise words, and ought to be well heeded.

Of course all Christians say, Bring the children into the Church; but how? and when? These are the practical questions. We have tried the pulpit-preaching and youthful season from twelve to twenty years, and we get in one in twenty or forty. The cradle and nursery season, with lessons and training adapted thereto, will succeed far better. It is a thousand times more natural, far more scriptural, and far more easy of accomplishment. Let teaching be properly directed, and mankind is never found so teachable as in the cradle and nursery. Such lessons are ingrain and lasting.

The foolishest thing ever dreamed of by unwise and indolent parents and their thoughtless friends is, "Let the children grow up unfettered, and choose Churches and Church-relation for themselves—I will not bind them in matters of conscience." Hear the Bishop again on this point: "How totally they misconceive the nature of the parental relation. The fact is that during infancy the parent *does every thing for the child*, and is obliged to do this by the very facts in the case. He must believe for the child, and act for him in every interest, even the most vital. The child is in his hands, incapable of acting for himself, and he must act for him, or let him perish. The responsibility is on him, and he cannot avoid it. What food the child shall eat, what atmosphere he shall live in, what medicine he shall take, the parent must determine. Nor does he make a title-deed in which he does not covenant for his child as well as for himself. If you say a man cannot choose for his child, you contradict nature itself and the customs of mankind from the earliest ages. If a man may not bind his child by covenant *in the matter of religion*, it is an exception to the authority he holds in all other relations. If this be so, an advantage is lost to the child *in this highest of all interests* that is secured to him in all other cases."

These are wise words, but our practice falls sadly short of the doctrine taught. We have very few children in the Church. Can we not improve in this matter? The children ought to be in the Church. I was glad to hear Bishop Andrew say, in connection with this subject, from the presiding-chair of the General Conference of 1870, that he never joined the Church—he never breathed out of it. It looks unnatural to see parents in the Church and their children out. Well-directed effort cannot fail of considerable improvement.

CHAPTER XXXIV.

A PRACTICAL SUGGESTION.

I HAVE long since been inclined to the belief that some change in the disposal of our regular ministerial labors might, and probably would, be beneficial to the cause of Christ. Is it certain that our ordinary pastoral labors are planned and adapted to the best possible advantage?

While I would by no means undervalue the regular public pulpit labors of our pastoral ministry, I cannot but think that a portion of those labors might be employed in fresher, more promising, and more fruitful fields.

Nine-tenths of our pulpit-preaching is to persons over sixteen years old, and four-fifths of it is to those over twenty; so our entire pulpit labor is directed to the reclamation of persons who have been from ten to forty years living in open, known, and willful rebellion against God and his laws. With these persons open and notorious irreligion has grown into a settled habit. This habit has become about as settled as the color of the Ethiopian's skin, or the spots of the leopard. Our preaching is therefore not so much against the corruptions of our nature and the sinfulness of sin as such, but against the hundred-fold additions thereto made by the ten thousand repetitions of resistance to the offers of salvation. The great difficulty in the conversion of sinners is not so much our moral disabilities inherited from a corrupt ancestry—though this is by no means generally, if ever, overestimated—but it is the additions thereto, a hundred or a thousand-fold multiplied, in each individual case, by a persistent and constant rebellion running along through years and years of sinful life. The average of means and labor required in the conversion of one person of twenty or forty would be found sufficient for the conversion of fifty or a hundred, if properly directed, at the age of even five or six years.

The disadvantage by loss of time is here far greater than that of the farmer who would begin to cultivate his corn after it begins to ripen, with the weeds higher than the corn. By neglect he has prepared for himself hard work and a sickly harvest. That this is somewhat our condition, is easily seen. Not over, or not much over, one in every hundred we preach to becomes a Christian after the age of twenty; and, like the corn, after having stood half his life-time or more among, and being crowded by, weeds rank and poisonous, and as tall as himself, a dwarfish stalk and small product are all that need be looked for.

Is this picture overdrawn? It is not half drawn; it will not more than half reach the actual historic facts. Let any man look around and see.

Now, the question is not only pertinent but vital, whether we cannot adapt and dispose our pastoral force in some plain, easy, practical way, harmonizing with nature and with Scripture, which will promise to secure at least some of these lost early advantages. It is a poor agriculturist who uses no implements suited to any weeds but those which are full-grown, or nearly so, large, hard, and deep-rooted. And are not our implements of religion mainly, if not uniformly, adapted to this class of weeds only?

The following suggestions may seem radical, or like taking too large a step at once. If radical, they are all the better for it. No healthful improvement in any thing is very valuable that is not radical. I know of nothing more radical than the gospel. As to taking a large step at once, if in the right direction it cannot be too large.

Suppose we at once discontinue one-fourth or more of our regular Sunday-preaching—say, ordinarily, have public service at church once on Sunday, the regular morning sermon, and public prayer-meeting once a week. Incidental and irregular worship need not perhaps be interfered with. Circuit preachers will conform as near as may be.

This relief from one-half his pulpit labor and preparation will give the pastor time for *regular pastoral family-preaching*, or "visiting," if that term be preferred. This family-preaching should be made regular and systematic. The visits would be generally, perhaps uniformly, appointed beforehand, and at times most agreeable to the family and the preacher. After prayer, reading the Scriptures, etc.—the children of course all being present—a half hour will be spent in explaining to the children, especially the smaller ones, the few great facts of Christianity, viz.: that Jesus, being the Christ of God, died for children to save them, loves them, will take them to heaven if they be good, etc.; that deceased children have gone to heaven if they were good; that to be good is to obey ma and pa, and mind quick; must not quarrel with little sister; and such simple, practical teaching as may be adapted to the understanding of the children severally, spending sufficient time with each one. Of course our Sunday-school literature will be interspersed and explained, referring to Sunday-school lessons, etc., and to the teachings of former visits. Scripture historic incidents will be introduced and impressed upon the little minds, and the whole visit made as interesting as possible. Particular attention will be paid to the smaller ones: children are so wonderfully—I know not but I might almost say miraculously—imitative that the lisping babes can be easily drawn into these religious lessons, if skillfully conducted; and thus with but little labor, with no flourish of splendid performance, and no great ado, a solid foundation for Christian character and Christian life may be secured, which can probably be done in no other way so well.

These family-preachings must not be incidental, occasional, or left at loose ends, but be regular, systematic, and have all the solemnity of the congregational Sunday-preaching. The children know when the preacher will be there again, they anticipate some of his inquiries, and will be ready to answer questions and rehearse lessons left them before, and will feel disappointed if by some accident the preacher does not come.

Of course, in all this the full, complete, and regular Church-membership of the children is supposed and recognized, and the children themselves are made to feel and appreciate it. This alone is a powerful advantage.

Now, who will venture to say that it is not probable, if not morally certain, that even a few family lessons of this kind, followed by suitable training, might not do more toward building up a solid Christian character, in any given instance, than a hundred sermons preached to the same person twenty years afterward, as we uniformly find such persons in their adult years? At least, I prayerfully believe the subject, further drawn out, explained, naturalized, and *Scripturized*, is worthy the serious consideration and examination of our sagest and wisest masters.

In these pastoral preachings the parents and older members of the family will by no means be left out of the account. The pastor will see that each family be furnished with a copy of *this book*, or a better one on the same subject, with recommendations, explanations, etc.; and in order to do which with proper advantage, he himself must be fully impressed with the great natural and constitutional truth that the little tiny teachings and habits of early childhood always and almost exclusively form the basis and staple of character throughout after-life.

We must, as well as possible, reach the mothers of our children with two great practical lessons: first, the vital necessity of establishing a habit of obedience in their children from the first; and, secondly, the ease with which this may be done. The difficulty is, just here, as is well known, that most, or perhaps I might say almost all, of these mothers themselves were badly trained, and know but little of what cheerful obedience is. Most of them know nothing about it. A mother evinces a disgraceful ignorance of children by declaring that this and that one never could be governed. She never tried it, and knows nothing about it. If she did not herself teach the child to govern her during the child's first year or two, she sat stupidly by and saw the ungovernable spirit rise and grow from a germ no stronger than a zephyr to the giant proportions of almost absolute sway, while she herself crouched in submission at the feet of an imperial suckling or prattler. We must, as well as we can, make mothers see and understand these simple and important things. We must make as many of them as we can understand that there is almost nothing so simple and easy of accomplishment as to establish a habit of happy, cheerful, ready obedience in any child, if set about and persevered in from the first; but that if attempted in any way short of *from the first*, it will be found an almost or quite fruitless undertaking.

We must reach the mothers through the children, and reach the children through the mothers. Prayer, patience, persistence, and perseverance, will accomplish wonders; and I can conceive of no more practical and promising mode than that suggested in this chapter, or something like it

It is questionable with me whether a discontinuance of one-half our public Sunday-preaching will much, if at all, lessen the good effects of that particular mode of ministering the gospel; and that the other half of the minister's time can be more profitably employed directly among the mothers and children at home, looks probable to me.

Our public preaching is too public, too general. It is adapted too much for everybody, and not enough for anybody. Much of it lacks specification and personality. There was great force and naturalness in Nathan's mode of preaching to David. "Thou art the man" is not difficult of comprehension.

Is it too much to say that our children get no preaching? It would hardly do to say that without some qualification. A few go to church occasionally — scarcely one in a hundred goes regularly; and when they go they hear very little they can understand. Almost all the sermons we hear nowadays are both calculated and intended for the most intelligent and best-informed portion of the congregation. The well-grown girls and boys, as well as the most uninformed part of the congregation, generally get but little preaching adapted to them, while the children of ten years and under get, it might almost be said, none.

I will at least ask this question, and bespeak for it some special attention at the hands of our bishops, and leading men of the Church, in and out of the ministry: Cannot some way be contrived by which the gospel can be practically and advantageously ministered to the children? Cannot they have practically, as well as nominally, the advantage of a portion of the labors of our pastoral ministry?

That our children now, in our present mode of working, have but very poor religious privileges, in proportion to our grown people, is the humiliating confession which the truth imperatively demands.

CHAPTER XXXV.

THE LORD'S SUPPER.

ANOTHER thing almost uniformly neglected among us is the bringing our children early to the Lord's Supper. I know of no class of persons more likely to be benefited by this Christian duty than children of five or six years. The exclamation, "That is entirely too young!" is made with no good reason. It is much easier to make an objection than to state a reason for it.

If the Christian duty and benefits of this sacrament were an open question, one of mere expediency, to be declined or adopted by each person for himself as he might judge best, then and in that case I could see reasons why a person should wait for adult years and opportunity to study theology and inquire into the reasons of it in its application to his particular case. But it is not such a case. The duty is absolute, and not subject to human opinion or revision.

"But surely a child should be old enough to

understand about it, and know what he is doing."

Yes, all that is necessary. You cannot communicate to a very young child any devotional idea, or but few ideas of any kind; you cannot tell him any thing about God, or Christ, or heaven. But the child of three years or so will soon begin to catch the devotional idea of blessing at table, and of family-prayer. He will mark the tone and solemn silence of the older children, and grasp the imitative idea. I may be permitted to suppose that in religious families children are seldom, if ever, permitted to reach the end of the fourth year, or probably the beginning of it, before the child is both taught and made accustomed to his little nursery-prayer. He understands what prayer *is* as well as the mother does. He has asked the Lord for his blessing and protection, and he confidently expects it.

Now, will any man say that a child of sufficient years and intelligence to understand prayer and participate profitably in it is not capable of understanding the Lord's Supper and of participating in it with equal probable profit? Is there more science or theology about the latter than the former? The child knows exactly what you tell him about each and both, and he knows no more. Tell him to pray his little tiny prayer, "Now I lay me down to sleep," and that the Lord will hear him and take care of him, and he believes it; and in like manner tell him the Lord said that all good people must take this sacrament to remember him, and he would love them more and take care of them better, and he believes that, and acts accordingly.

And how much more than that does the parent or the pastor know? Did we discover prayer and the Lord's Supper by learning, science, or human knowledge? Who knows more about it than a child of five or six years can be told and understand? Beyond this simple elementary knowledge level to the comprehension of a child, the learned doctors are not agreed to-day. The Lord's Supper is an outward, formal, ceremonial acknowledgment of subserviency and obligation to God, commanded by Christ. The man who knows more than that about it has learned more than I have.

Bishop Marvin talks so well along here—let us hear him again:

"My neighbor says, 'I will not bind my child in the affairs of his soul. He shall be *free*. He shall *choose for himself*.' This is quite taking to the popular ear.

"But I say my child shall not be free to go wrong, either in religion or any thing else, if I can help it—and the more especially in religion than in any thing else. I will bind him by commands, by covenants, and by all the most sacred obligations, to serve God. I will environ him with motives that he shall feel it to be unnatural and monstrous for him to disregard. I will make it in the highest degree difficult and painful for him to go to hell.

"To this view of the case the Church must be brought. There is much need of light among us. Our Church needs toning up greatly on this subject. Thousands in the Church use little effort to turn the young, unpracticed feet of their children from the way of death."

In the particular case now before us nothing is needed but a little encouraging counsel and example. How much of this is done among us? I will ask the first pastor I meet, How often have you talked plainly to parents and children on the subject? How often have you explained to both that all that was necessary for a child to know, or understand, about the Lord's Supper, in order to a proper participation in it, is that Jesus directed it to be done in order that we might the better remember that he died for us?

Is that a difficult and abstruse lesson in theology for a child to learn? I never administered this sacrament in my life with more satisfaction and solemnity than to children of five or six years. My grief has been that there were so few. I want to see the children grow up in this nurture and admonition. Keep them in it. Why let them go out, lest they stay out? Verily, Bishop, our Church needs toning up on this subject.

What can look more lovely or more Christian than to see a parent or elder brother or sister leading the little one to the sacramental altar, where they both, or the whole family, kneel together in public ceremonial remembrance of the Lord of the Church? It is in this way that our little ones become sacredly familiar with the Church and its duties. Its ceremonies and services become interwoven into the very texture of the child's thoughts and feelings, and make up his practical religious being.

I am indebted for lessons along here respecting the children of the Church to one of the young preachers of the district where I was presiding elder years ago. He had more children and smaller ones on his Church-register than any other pastor—sometimes' more than all the rest of the district; and he had more children and smaller ones at his prayer-meetings and at the Lord's table than any of the rest. And I asked myself, How is this? And I soon saw how it was.

Let the bishops "tone up," and let presiding elders and pastors tone up. Verily, the Church needs toning up.

If the foregoing observations are sound, they ought to be acted out in the Church. To inaugurate these things into a practical working system may require time and labor. I think it will be generally admitted that the theory is pretty correctly stated—substantially stated at least—as far as stated at all. The practical work requires the whole working machinery of the Church. Will our bishops and leading ministers consider the propriety and expediency of bringing our children fully and practically into the Church? And will not the entire Church, pastors and people, wake up to a more true, natural, and apostolic system of Christian Cradlehood? May the God of heaven spur our energies and stimulate our zeal!

CONCLUSION.

IT seems to me that under a good system of nursery-training and discipline our ministerial force could be made far more efficient than it now is. Our ministrations are now for the most part, may be three-fourths or twice that amount, employed in the undoing of habits formed and character established not by Adam, as many vainly suppose, but by ourselves. Adam is charged with a thousand things of which we ourselves are guilty. Our condition at birth, call it by what name you will, may be set down to the account of Adam, or *original* sin; but not the condition of the boy or girl of five, ten, or twenty years, or the man or woman of forty. This great increase of wickedness must be charged to our own account. We have added to the "original" stock of moral depravity, or sinfulness—call it by what name you will—perhaps forty or five hundred-fold. This difference between the "original" stock and the present amount may not be exactly measurable by us, as we have not the means of doing it, but it is as plainly observable as a mountain is distinguishable from a mole-hill. A young child has a tendency, disposition, or inclination, to sin, but no actual sin. When grown to sinful capability, the child has added to this tendency a vast amount of accumulated guilt. His corruption has grown largely. To estimate this difference, or to ascertain how much of the corruption of a person of ten or twenty years is new, and how much old, we must compare the condition of the new-born infant with the advanced person. Suppose this difference to be tenfold—which is no doubt generally very far below the truth—then one-tenth part of all our ministerial labor is employed in the eradication of the natural and unavoidable corrupt condition of our fellow-men, and nine-tenths against the additions we ourselves have willfully and wickedly made to it. Let us face the truth fairly.

Then, one-tenth part—but really more likely it is one-hundredth part—of the general wickedness around us is inherited capital to begin with, and to this we have added, by our own conduct and criminal negligence, the other nine-tenths, or ninety-nine hundredths. Now, the question arises, Had we not better turn our labors, or a portion of them, against this large increase of accumulated stock in the way of preventive? Prevention is better than cure. Can we not get control of this rapidly increasing stream of guilt at or near the fountain? Sin is *never necessary*. Then, it is *always eradicable*. The argument in the foregoing treatise recommends that we move our works nearer the fountain—as near as we can get—and not wait till the stream has acquired large volume and heavy momentum. I think the practicability of ministering the gospel to the inhabitants of the cradle and the nursery has been shown. The gospel is adapted to persons of all ages, and not by any means exclusively to those of five or ten years and upward. The child of one year, or the half of it, is capable of obedience, as much so as he ever will be; and from that time on a habit of cheerful, ready obedience is easily established and maintained. His obedience is to what he recognizes as rightful authority. In a very short time, as the intellect begins to open a little, and he can begin to understand a little about Bible characters, and God, and Christ, this obedience is easily extended from the parent to the Maker. Christianity is exactly adapted to the particular condition of every person at every period of life from the birth to the grave, and to no one period better than another.

17

The largest difficulty in the way, outside of ourselves probably, is the irreligious associations to which our children are necessarily exposed. If this cannot be wholly, it can be partially, overcome by care and diligence. If parents expect to bring up children for any good, they must expect to do something more than supply their physical wants. The parental relation implies constant, unceasing labor and care to keep the little ones from ruinous troubles with which this world is so full. Both pastor and parent must double, treble—yea, quadruple—not the amount of labor bestowed on children, but the amount of well-directed thought and care so appreciated. The pastor has as yet scarcely entered this field. There is an open door and high promise of rich harvest.

THE END.

www.ingramcontent.com/pod-product-compliance
Lightning Source LLC
Chambersburg PA
CBHW021349230426
43666CB00006B/456